WAR,
WOMEN,
AND
DRUIDS

BY PHILIP FREEMAN

WAR, WOMEN, AND DRUIDS

EYEWITNESS REPORTS AND EARLY ACCOUNTS OF THE ANCIENT CELTS

University of Texas Press, Austin

Requests for permission to reproduce material from this work
should be sent to Permissions, University of Texas Press,
P.O. Box 7819, Austin, TX 78713-7819.

♾ The paper used in this book meets the minimum
requirements of ANSI/NISO Z39.48-1992 (R1997)
(Permanence of Paper).

Library of Congress Cataloging-in-Publication Data

Freeman, Philip, 1961–
War, women, and druids : eyewitness reports and early
accounts of the ancient Celts / by Philip Freeman.—1st ed.
        p.   cm.
Includes bibliographical references and index.
ISBN 0-292-72545-0 (alk. paper)
1. Civilization, Celtic—Sources. 2. Druids and
Druidism—Sources. 3. Celts—Europe—Sources.
4. Celts—Religion—Sources. 5. Women, Celtic—Sources.
                I. Title.
              D70 .F74 2002
    936.4—dc21   2002002779

For my mother and father

CONTENTS

PREFACE

The ancient Celts capture the modern imagination as do few other people of classical times. Naked barbarians charging the Roman legions, Druids performing sacrifices of unspeakable horror, women fighting beside their men and even leading armies—these, along with stunning works of art, are the images most of us call to mind when we think of the Celts. And for the most part, these images are firmly based in the descriptions handed down to us by the Greek and Roman writers.

As with historical sources from any age, we cannot accept at face value everything the classical authors say about the Celts and we must always approach their words with caution. Every ancient (and modern) writer has particular motives and prejudices, even when they are attempting to portray an honest picture of Celtic life. Some authors, such as Julius Caesar, are anxious to present a brave and noble—if somewhat peculiar— enemy in order to enhance their own achievements in conquering them. Other writers seek to show the Celts as noble savages embodying the high moral philosophy lost in Roman culture. On the other hand, some delight in portraying the Celts as disgusting barbarians desperately in need of a good dose of civilization. But most ancient authors are simply trying to record as accurately as possible for their own various purposes what they have seen, heard, or read of Celtic life.

Even with these shortcomings, the writings of the Greeks and Romans are our primary source of information on the ancient Celts. Archaeology has unearthed beautiful works of art and revealed much about Celtic culture, but nothing can replace the testimony of contemporary witnesses. In this book I try to present that testimony clearly to all interested readers. I have kept the introductory comments to the passages at a minimum in order to let the Greeks and Romans speak for themselves about the Celts. In my translations of the original sources, whether Greek or Latin, I have always tried to be faithful to the texts, but sometimes a loose translation or even paraphrase of the original author best conveys the meaning to modern readers.

The final chapter contains translations of inscriptions written by the ancient Celts themselves rather than the Greeks or Romans. These sources are limited and often are poorly understood even by specialists, but they provide a unique glimpse of ancient Celtic life through the words of those who lived it.

I have avoided the scholarly temptation to add tedious footnotes to every section, though a list of secondary sources is included at the end of the book for readers seeking to learn more about the fascinating world of the ancient Celts.

I owe many thanks to those experts in Classical and Celtic studies who read the manuscript of this book, especially Patrick Ford, Joseph Eska, John Carey, Pamela Hopkins, Katherine Forsyth, Thomas Clancy, Jerry Hunter, and Barbara Hillers.

WAR,
WOMEN,
AND
DRUIDS

Ireland

Britain

Celtic Lands
of Western Europe

ATLANTIC OCEAN

Gaul

Cisalpine
Gaul

Celtiberia

ROME

DELPHI

WAR

The Greeks and Romans viewed the Celts above all else as warriors *par excellence*. Very often the first experience any part of the classical world had with the Celts was the terrifying sight of a Celtic army approaching with giant swords drawn and screaming naked warriors leading the way. For the Romans, the Celts were the barbarians who almost destroyed their city in 390 B.C. and the relentless enemy they faced at every turn as they expanded across Europe for the next four hundred years. The Greeks knew them first as the invaders who threatened their homeland in the third century B.C., then as the Galatians who ravaged and eventually settled in nearby Asia Minor. Even when the Celts were finally tamed, they were highly valued as mercenaries in the Greek east and as soldiers in the legions of Rome.

* * *

The earliest source on Celtic warfare is the Greek historian Xenophon writing *c.* 360 B.C. His two passages on the subject are short and provide no information about Celtic techniques of fighting, but they do show that the Celts were valued mercenary soldiers in the classical world. In this case, Dionysius, tyrant of Syracuse in Sicily, hired Celtic mercenaries and transported them to Greece in 369 B.C. to aid his Spartan allies (*Hellenica* 7.1.20):

At this time an auxiliary force from Dionysius arrived to help the Spartans. The force consisted of more than twenty ships and carried Celts, Iberians, and about fifty cavalry.

The next year, another group of Celtic mercenaries arrived from Dionysius and helped the Spartans repel a surprise attack with such ferocity that neither the Celts nor their allies suffered any casualties (7.1.31):

The rest were slain while they ran away, many by the cavalry and many also by the Celts.

* * *

A fragmentary inscription from the Acropolis in Athens dated 352/1 B.C. shows that Celtic weapons were valued by the Greeks at an early date. This list of arms dedicated to the goddess Athena includes some of Celtic origin (*Inscriptiones Graecae* ii² 1438):

> Copper helmets from Argos . . .
> 261 assorted copper armaments and royal tiaras . . .
> Celtic weapons of iron.

* * *

The fourth-century B.C. philosopher Aristotle mentions the martial qualities of the Celts several times. He first uses the Celts as an example of excess in his famous defense of moderation. He says that an excessive amount of any quality, even bravery, is not desirable (*Nichomachean Ethics* 3.7):

For the sake of honor, a virtuous man will stand his ground and perform brave deeds. But as we have noted before, there is no name for those who carry this sort of quality to the extreme, being absolutely without fear, not even being afraid of earthquakes or waves, as they say of the Celts.

He also mentions a supposedly widespread custom among non-Greeks of hardening children to adverse weather as training for war (*Politics* 15.2):

It is a commendable practice to accustom children to the cold from an early age. It is beneficial not only for reasons of health but also in view to future military service. This is why so many barbarian nations, such as the Celts, will dip their babies into cold rivers or give their children little clothing to wear.

Aristotle is also the first classical author to mention homosexual relations among Celtic warriors (*Politics* 2.6):

The result of ignoring women in law codes is that wealth will be overly desired in such a state, especially if women run things behind the scenes as in most military societies. An exception to this would be those nations which openly approve of sexual relations between men, such as the Celts and certain others.

* * *

Aristotle's contemporary Ephorus includes in his *History*, now lost except for references in later authors, an amusing but practical note on physical fitness among Celtic warriors (Strabo *Geography* 4.4.6):

Ephorus says that the Celts are very careful not to become fat or potbellied. If any young man's belly sticks over his belt he is punished.

* * *

Another fourth-century B.C. Greek writer shows a more cunning side of Celtic warfare. In his now lost *History of Philip*, parts of which are preserved in Athenaeus, Theopompus records a deadly trick played on the Illyrians by their Celtic foes (Athenaeus *Deipnosophistae* 10.443):

The Celts, knowing that the Illyrians loved to indulge themselves at feasts, invited them all to a great banquet in their tents. But they put a certain herb in the food which immediately attacked their bowels and produced mass diarrhea. The Celts then captured and slew some of them while others threw themselves into rivers, unable to stand the pain.

* * *

Alexander the Great's general Ptolemy records in his fragmentary history a meeting between some Celts and young Alexander during a campaign in Thrace in 335 B.C. The Celts' answer to Alexander's question bears a remarkable resemblance to the oath taken before battle by Irish warriors in the medieval *Táin Bó Cúailnge* epic: "We shall hold this ground where we stand.

Unless the earth quakes or the sky falls on us, we shall not be moved" (Strabo *Geography* 7.3.8):

Ptolemy son of Lagus says that some Celts living near the Adriatic Sea arrived during this war and sought a treaty of friendship with Alexander. He welcomed them and while they were sharing a drink asked them what they feared the most, thinking they would say him. But they answered that they feared nothing except the sky falling down on them, though they did value the friendship of a man such as him above all else.

* * *

In 279 B.C., the Celts of the northern Balkans erupted into Greece. The invasion was described by Pompeius Trogus, a writer of Gaulish origin drawing on earlier sources, several centuries later during the reign of Augustus and collected in digest form by Justin in the second or third century A.D. (*Epitome* 24.6–8):

Brennus was the leader of the Gauls who had poured into Greece. When he heard that Belgius had led the Gauls to victory over the Macedonians then abandoned the rich plunder swollen with goods from the east, he was so angry that he collected together an army of one hundred and fifty thousand infantry and fifteen thousand cavalry and invaded Macedonia himself. While pillaging the Macedonian countryside, he was met by Sosthenes at the head of a Macedonian army. But the Macedonians were few and frightened while the Gauls were numerous and unafraid, so that they had an easy victory. The Macedonians then hid inside their walled cities while Brennus and the invading Gauls looted the entire countryside unopposed. Then as if the spoils of men were not enough for him, he turned his attention to the temples of the immortal gods, joking foolishly that they were generous and ought to share their goods with men. Immediately he turned the army towards Delphi, setting plunder before piety and gold before fear of the gods.

When Brennus came within sight of the temple at Delphi, he debated for a long time whether he should attack immediately or give his troops the night to rest first. The leaders of the Aenians and the

Thessalians, who had joined his plundering army, urged that there be no delay—attack while the enemy was unprepared and frightened still by the arrival of the Gauls. If he allowed the night to pass, then the people of Delphi would regain their courage, perhaps recruit allies, and blockade roads which were yet open. But the Gaulish soldiers, who had traveled a long distance without decent food or drink, soon discovered that the countryside around Delphi was well supplied with food and wine. This made them as happy as if they had already won a victory. They broke into marauding bands and seized all the goods they could find. This gave the people of Delphi the time they needed. They say that when the Gauls had first approached Delphi, the oracles had forbidden them to move their crops and wine out of their country houses. No one understood the reason for this injunction until the delay caused by the ransacking Gauls allowed the Delphians to recruit allies from nearby towns. The people of Delphi and their allies then strengthened the defenses of their town while the Gauls lay around drinking wine as if it were the spoils of victory. Once Brennus managed to collect together some troops, he had sixty-five thousand infantry compared to the four thousand soldiers defending Delphi. The Gaulish leader scoffed at such puny numbers and roused his men by pointing out the many statues and chariots visible—solid gold, he said, more plunder than you can even imagine.

The Gauls were thrilled at such a prospect and, even though they were suffering terribly from the wild night of drinking, they plunged into battle caring nothing for danger. The Delphians meanwhile despised the Gauls and trusted more in Apollo than in their strength. They hurled down spears and rocks on the advancing Gauls who were climbing towards them. In the middle of the battle, priests burst out of the temples wearing their robes and regalia, hair disheveled, shouting that they had seen the god Apollo himself leaping down into his temple while they were crying to him for help. Two beautiful virgins, Diana and Minerva, had joined him from nearby temples. Not only had they seen them, they claimed, but they had heard the sound of the bow and the clash of weapons. Thus they urged the people of Delphi not to hesitate but to slaughter the enemy in the very presence of the gods.

The Delphians were encouraged by these claims and attacked the Gauls with great abandon. Everyone soon felt the presence of the god as a part of the mountain itself fell on top of the Gauls and the firm lines of the Greeks drove them away. A hailstorm then arose which finished off the wounded. Brennus himself was unable to stand the pain of his wounds and killed himself with his dagger, while one of the Gaulish leaders punished those who had advocated the attack and led the surviving ten thousand troops limping out of Greece. But it was a miserable retreat for the Gauls. Day and night they were exposed to the elements, faced constant danger and hardship, suffered unceasing rain, biting snow, hunger, and worst of all, fatigue wore down the sad remnants of the Gaulish army. In the lands through which they passed they were harassed and attacked constantly by the native population, so that the Gauls, a short while ago so confident that they attacked the gods themselves, were destroyed with none surviving to tell the tale of their great disaster.

* * *

Other branches of the invading Gauls crossed into Asia Minor (modern Turkey) and ravaged the land for decades before settling down as the Galatians of central Anatolia. The contemporary writer Callimachus, one of the most famous of Hellenistic poets, reflects the general terror these Celts inspired among the Greeks (*Hymn* 4).

> And one day in the future a common fight will come upon us,
> when against the Greeks
> later-born Titans among the war-crazed Celts
> shall raise a barbarian sword,
> rushing headlong from the farthest West.

* * *

One place in Asia Minor attacked by the Gauls was the Greek city of Miletus, sacked about 277 B.C. A poem of the same era, traditionally ascribed to Anyte, describes with a melodramatic flair the choice made by three young virgins trapped in the city. Although the poem is probably nothing but fiction, it portrays the very real fear felt by the Greeks facing these barbarian invaders from the west (*Greek Anthology* 7.492):

O Miletus, dear home, we leave you now,
fleeing the uncivilized passion of the godless Gauls,
three maidens, citizens, whom the savage violence
of the Celts forced to this sad fate.
For we would not consent to such an impious joining
nor wedding, but we chose a union with Hades.

* * *

The Galatians of Asia Minor eventually ceased ransacking Greek cities and settled down, but they did not lose their martial abilities. In fact they became valued mercenaries throughout the eastern Mediterranean. Justin preserves, in condensed form, early accounts of these eastern Celts written by contemporary Greek historians (*Epitome* 25.2):

At that time the population growth of the Galatians was so great that they filled Asia like some kind of swarm. Finally none of the eastern kings would wage any war without these Celtic mercenaries.

* * *

The Romans long remembered the Gaulish sack of their city in 390 B.C. In time, a great deal of myth grew up around the event, but the historian Livy in the late first century B.C. does draw on early historical sources in his description (5.41):

At Rome, preparations had been made for defending the high ground of the Capitol Hill, so the old men who had chosen to die returned to their homes to face death with a brave spirit. Those who had been consuls or held other high office in the government put on the robes they wore to bear the images of the gods at the games or to celebrate their triumphal parades. They then seated themselves in the ivory chairs of office in the middle of their homes. Some historians say that Marcus Folius, the chief priest, led them in a prayerful chant in which they devoted themselves to death on behalf of their country and people.

The lust of the Gauls for battle meanwhile had been cooled by a night of rest. The previous fight had not been much of a struggle and now the city lay open and unguarded before them. They entered the city through the open Colline Gate and inspected the Forum. They noticed that the Capitol was defended, so they posted guards around it to prevent any attack on their scattered forces while they sacked the city. They rushed through the empty streets, some to whatever house was nearest and others to more distant homes thinking these would have more to offer. But the houses were unnerving by their very emptiness and silence and, fearing some sort of trap, the Gauls returned in time to the area of the Forum. There the houses of the plebeians were shut up tightly, but those of the nobles stood open. They were almost more afraid to enter the open houses as they saw in the vestibules seated men who seemed to them to be like gods. It was more than just the splendid way these old men were dressed—their very bearing and dignity seemed more godlike than human. The Gauls stared at the seated men as if they were statues until, it is said, one of the barbarians touched the beard (the fashion then) of Marcus Papirius—at which point the Roman hit him on the head with his ivory staff. This broke the spell and roused the Gauls to anger. Marcus Papirius was killed and the rest of the nobles were massacred where they sat. No one was spared as the houses were ransacked and burned to the ground.

* * *

The second-century B.C. Greek historian Polybius provides the earliest extensive description of the Celts at war. In the many books of his *Histories*, he chronicles the rise of Rome as a world power and includes carefully researched descriptions of Roman battles with the Celts of northern Italy. In 225 B.C., the Celtic tribes of Cisalpine Gaul banded together, along with forces imported from Transalpine Gaul, to plunder parts of Italy, but were forced into an unwanted battle with the Romans near the town of Telamon in Etruria, midway between Rome and Pisa. The defeat of the Gauls at the Battle of Telamon marked the end of Celtic military power south of the Alps (2.28–31):

The Cisalpine Celts, along with the Gaesatae from beyond the Alps and the Insubres, drew up their forces on and near a hill to face the Roman general Aemilius, while the Taurisci and Boii from the right bank of the Po River faced the opposite direction to confront the legions of the consul Gaius. They positioned their wagons and chariots at both ends of the forces and moved all the plunder they had gathered during their raids to a nearby hill surrounded by guards. This arrangement of the Celts in a battle array facing in both directions not only looked fearsome but was well suited to the threat they faced. The Insubres and the Boii wore pants and light cloaks, but the proud Gaesatae had thrown off all their clothes and stood naked facing the Romans, both out of brash confidence in their own abilities and for the practical reason that they did not want their clothes to snag on the brambles covering the ground and impede the use of their weapons. At first the battle was fought only on the hill with the great number of cavalry from both sides clashing there furiously. The consul Gaius, after a heroic struggle, was killed at this point in the battle and his head was brought to the Celtic leaders.

But at last the Roman cavalry stubbornly forced their way upwards and captured the hill. Now the infantry of both sides faced each other in a battle remarkable not only to those who were present but also to those who imagined it afterwards from the reports of witnesses. Again, both those who fought in the battle and those who report it cannot be certain if the Celts were at an advantage or disadvantage in their unusual arrangement as they fought Romans on two sides and at the same time protected the backs of their comrades. Moreover, their two-faced formation cut off all possibility of retreat and hope of escape if they were defeated. The Romans for their part were both thrilled at having trapped the Celtic forces between two armies and absolutely terrified by the sight of their finely arrayed forces and the tremendous clamor. For the Celts had numerous horn players and trumpeters blowing at full might, while at the same time the shouting and war cries of the warriors themselves raised such a din that it seemed to the Romans as if the whole surrounding countryside was alive and screaming at them.

The sight and movements of the naked warriors in the front of the battle lines were also terrifying, for the Celts were all young, powerfully built men wearing gold torques on their necks and gleaming bands on their arms. On the other hand, the Romans were eager to defeat these men and win such spoils for themselves.

The Roman spearmen advanced from their lines and began to throw their weapons at the enemy. The Celts in the rear were protected somewhat by their pants and cloaks, but the naked warriors who were fighting in front suffered terribly, for the Gaulish shield does not cover the whole body in a fight, so that those who were the biggest and most exposed were being injured the worst. Finally, as they were unable to drive back the spearmen due to their distance and the continuous rain of their spears, some of the Gauls began to charge the Romans in a wild, suicidal fury, while others retreated slowly and threw their comrades into confusion and despair. So the spirit of the Gaesatae was broken by the Roman spearmen, but the Insubres, Boii, and Taurisci continued the fight in vicious hand-to-hand combat after the spearmen had withdrawn. Though they were being slaughtered in the battle, they held their ground, equal to the Romans in courage, but inferior in weapons. The Roman shields offered much greater protection, while Gaulish swords were not good for thrusting, only for swinging wide and slashing. At the end, the Roman cavalry charged down from the hill, driving away the Gaulish horsemen and cutting their infantry to pieces.

About forty thousand Gaulish warriors were slain at Telamon, including the chieftain Concolitanos. Another leader, Aneroestes, escaped with a few followers to a certain place where they all committed suicide. The Roman general collected together the spoils and sent them ahead to Rome, returning to the rightful owners the booty the Gauls had previously taken. He then led the army into the Ligurian lands of the Boii and allowed the legions to pillage there as much as they wanted. Then they all returned to Rome. The general sent the Gaulish banners and torques (the gold necklaces worn by the Celts) to the Capitol, but he used the rest of the spoils and the prisoners of war as ornaments in his triumphal parade.

* * *

The second-century B.C. Latin poet Lucilius gives one of the earliest Roman descriptions of Celtic warriors in his fragmentary poetry. The subjects here are probably the Celtiberians of Spain (Nonius *De compendiosa doctrina* 227.33):

> They were a beautiful sight
> with colorful cloaks and pants
> and huge torques on their necks.

The Greek Stoic philosopher Posidonius traveled widely in Gaul at the beginning of the first century B.C. conducting ethnographic research. His work is lost to modern readers, but he was used as a prime source on the Celts by other ancient writers such as Diodorus Siculus, Strabo, and Athenaeus. Even secondhand, Posidonius' reports on the Gauls are of great value, as the philosopher was a careful observer of Celtic life in the decades just before the Roman conquest—a time when Gaul was still an untamed land belonging to Celts alone.

* * *

Diodorus preserves Posidonius' description of Gaulish warfare and the gruesome custom of keeping heads as battle trophies (5.29):

For journeys and in battles the Gauls use a two-horse chariot which carries both a driver and a warrior who stands beside him. When they meet cavalry in war, they hurl their spears then jump off the chariot and fight with their swords. Some of them are so unafraid of death that they come into the battle naked except for a loincloth. The Gauls use free men of the poorer classes in war as charioteers and shield bearers. When the warriors face each other on the field of battle, one will often go in front of his companions and challenge the best of the other side to single combat while showing off his weapons and trying to fill his opponents with fear. If someone accepts his challenge, he will begin boasting about the courage of his ancestors and describing his own brave deeds while mocking and belittling his challenger, all in an attempt to destroy his opponent's courage with words.

The Gauls cut off the heads of their enemies killed in battle and hang them from their horses' necks. They take the bloodstained weapons and spoils from their dead enemies and give them to their servants while they sing a song of victory. These spoils they hang up on their houses like hunting trophies. The heads of their enemies they then preserve in cedar oil, storing them carefully in chests. They will proudly show these to visiting strangers and relate how an ancestor or their father or they themselves turned down a large sum of money for the head. Some of them, in a strange kind of arrogance, even say they have turned down an equal weight in gold! In my opinion, such actions are not a mark of virtue but a sign of barbarity, since even wild beasts don't continue to make war on dead enemies.

Diodorus continues with a description of Gaulish clothing, armor and weapons (5.30):

The clothing of the Gauls is striking. They wear long shirts dyed in various colors and pants which they call bracae. They also wear striped cloaks fastened at the neck, thick in winter and light in the summer. These are also decorated with patterns of tightly packed squares. Their armor includes oblong shields the height of a man embellished in various individual styles. Some of the shields have images of bronze animals which stick out and serve not only as decoration but also for protection. They also wear helmets with large figures on top, making the wearer look even taller and more fearsome. Some of these helmets have horns projecting from them, but others have the front parts of birds or four-footed beasts. The trumpets they use in battle have a uniquely harsh and particularly barbaric sound perfectly suited for war. Some of the Gauls have chain-mail breastplates while others fight naked, using only the protection given them by nature. They use a broadsword instead of a smaller weapon and this hangs from their right side by an iron or bronze chain. Some of them wear a gold or silver-plated belt around their long shirts. The spears they use in battle have heads of iron eighteen inches or more in length and as wide as two palms put together. Gaulish swords are as long as the spears of other peoples and their spears have heads longer than most swords. Some of their spears have straight heads, but others have notched spiral heads which not only cut the flesh upon entry but tear it as well. Pulling this kind of spear head out rips the flesh horribly and makes the wound worse.

The first-century A.D. Greek writer Strabo also draws on the Posidonian tradition for the Gaulish section of his description of the world (*Geography* 4.4.2, 5):

All of the Gauls, who are called both Gallic and Galatian, are absolutely mad about war. They are high-spirited and quickly seek out a fight, but on the other hand they are sincere and not at all malicious. On account of this, they will come together quickly for combat if provoked without any attempt to hide their movements and without first making any plan for action, so that anyone who uses strategy can defeat them. If you wish to provoke them for any reason at any time, they will immediately respond to the danger without any fore-thought, attacking you with brute force and courage. But if you urge and coax them gently, they can quickly be educated and trained in language skills. Their reputation in war comes largely from their great size and huge population. They will come together rapidly in great numbers on account of their simple and straightforward concern for their countrymen who they believe have been treated unjustly. At the present time they live peacefully as subjects of Roman law, but I am taking this description from an earlier time and from the current cus-toms of the untamed Germanic tribes.

In addition to their simple and high-spirited nature, they also possess a lack of seriousness and a love of boasting along with a great affec-tion for ornaments. They wear golden jewelry such as necklaces and bracelets around their arms and wrists, while the upper classes wear dyed clothing decorated with gold. Because of their lightness in char-acter, they are both unbearable to be around when they are victorious and panic-stricken when things go against them. Beyond this sort of simplicity, they also practice a barbaric and uncivilized custom com-mon to many northern tribes—they hang the heads of their slain en-emies from the necks of their horses when they leave a battlefield and then hang them up on a peg when they get home. Posidonius says that he often saw this practice himself and was disgusted by it at first, but got used to it in time.

* * *

Caesar's *Gallic War*, describing his conquest of Gaul during the years 58–51 B.C., is a singularly important source of informa-tion about ancient Celtic life, especially conduct in war. Caesar was a brilliant tactician and general whose descriptions of his Gaulish enemies are generally fair and accurate. He gives them credit when due—which certainly makes the description of his ultimate triumph over them more impressive to his readers.

The war began as a result of threatening movements by the Gaulish Helvetii tribe of modern Switzerland into the Roman provincial territory in southern Gaul (modern Provence) and ended with the defeat of the general Vercingetorix and his army of united Gaul several years later.

Caesar begins his book with a sweeping description of Gaulish geography and tribes (1.1):

Gaul as a whole is divided into three parts—one is inhabited by the Belgae, another by the Aquitani, and the third by those called in their own language Celts, but in Latin Gauls. All of these differ from each other in language, social institutions, and laws. The Gauls are separated from the Aquitani by the Garonne River and from the Belgae by the Marne and Seine. Of all of these peoples, the Belgae are the most courageous because they are most distant from the civilizing influence of Rome. They are also seldom visited by Roman merchants bringing commodities which weaken the spirit. Proximity to the Germans with their constant fighting also toughens the Belgae considerably. The Helvetii are markedly brave for the same reason—almost daily battles with the Germans who border them, with the Germans raiding their lands and Gaulish counterattacks against German territory.

The Helvetii soon began to feel that their territory was too small to contain their numbers and determined to move west in search of better lands. To their misfortune, the best route lay through Roman territory—and Caesar was not about to allow thousands of well-armed Gaulish warriors safe passage through Roman lands. Nor would he allow the general disruption caused by such movement to cause disorder and devastation among the Gaulish tribes living outside of Roman lands but friendly to Rome. Thus the two armies met in the first battle of the Gallic War at Bibracte in east-central France (1.24–27):

When Caesar noticed that the Helvetii were following his troops and harassing them, he positioned his infantry on the nearest hill and sent his cavalry to stop the enemy's movement. He then positioned his four legions of veterans in a triple line halfway up the hill, but placed the two legions of troops recently recruited in Cisalpine Gaul and the auxiliary soldiers on the top of the ridge to fill the entire area of the hill with men. He also collected together the packs into one place guarded with trenches by the men on the high ground. The Helvetii followed the Romans and collected all their carts and baggage into one place. The Gaulish warriors pressed against the Roman cavalry in a densely packed line and forced them back, then moved up the hill against the nearest Roman line.

The first thing Caesar did was to send all the horses away, including his own, so that the danger would be the same for all and no one would be tempted to desert. Then the battle began. The Roman soldiers on the high ground easily scattered the massed formation of the Helvetii with a rain of spears, then they drew their swords and charged downhill. The Gauls had a great disadvantage at this point in the fight because many of them had several shields pierced and stuck together by one spear throw—with the spear bent and unable to be removed. They could not fight well with their shield arm so encumbered, so after shaking the shields in a vain effort to clear up this mess, many of them threw away their shields and fought without protection. Finally, after being worn down with wounds, they began to retreat, falling back to a hill about a mile away. There they began to recover themselves, but the legions soon followed. The allied Boii and Tulingi tribes, forming the rear guard with about fifteen thousand men, turned on the exposed side of the Romans and began to surround them. Then the Helvetii on the hill saw this and renewed their own attack, but the Romans split and started a two-pronged attack against both the Helvetii and their allies.

This battle in two directions was long and fierce. Finally, when the Gauls could no longer stand up to the Romans, one part retreated up the mountain while the rest moved back to protect the supplies in their carts. They were a brave enemy—throughout the whole battle lasting from midday until sunset, no Roman ever saw the back of a Gaulish warrior. Around the baggage carts, the fight lasted well into the night, since it was protected by a wall. From these heights the Gauls continuously rained down spears and even wounded the Romans from their positions between the carts and behind the wheels. But finally the legions captured the Gaulish supplies and camp. The daughter of the Helvetii leader Orgetorix and one of his sons were captured, but some one hundred and thirty thousand Gauls survived the battle and escaped. They marched all night and three days later reached the lands of the Lingones tribe to the north. The Romans were unable to follow them immediately because so many were wounded and dead. Caesar sent a message to the Lingones saying that if they gave any food to his enemies, then he would deal with them the same way as the Helvetii. And after three days, he followed them. So the Helvetii, finally, without supplies and with hope gone, sent ambassadors to Caesar seeking terms for their surrender.

But this was the beginning, not the end, of the war between the Gauls and Romans. For the next seven years, Caesar moved around the country subduing tribes, making treaties, then often subduing the tribes again after they rebelled. The Gauls finally learned that their only hope in defeating the Romans was to band together and fight as a nation instead of as individual tribes. Most tribes sent troops under Commius to relieve the besieged leader Vercingetorix at the surrounded city of Alesia, only a few miles north of the first battle site at Bibracte, and to finally drive the Romans out of Gaul (7.75–81):

The Gauls summoned a council of tribal leaders and decided not to send all the available troops to Vercingetorix, as he had requested, but only a certain number from each of the tribes. This was because they feared that such a large number would be impossible to keep under control, to keep divided into separate tribal groups, and to feed. So thirty-five thousand came from the Aedui and their allies the Segusiavi, Ambivareti, Aulerci Brannovices, and Blannovii. The same number was sent from the Arverni and their supporters, the Eleuteti, Cadurci, Gabali, and Vellavii. From the Sequani, Senones, Bituriges, Santoni, Ruteni, and Carnutes came twelve thousand each. Ten thousand troops arrived each from the Bellovaci and Lemovices. Eight thousand each from the Pictones, Turoni, Parisii, and Helvetii, with five thousand each from the Suessiones, Ambiani, Mediomatrici, Petrocorii, Nervii, Moroni, Nitiobriges, and Aulerci Cenomani. Four thousand came from the Atrebates and three thousand each from the Veliocasses, Lexovii, and Aulerci Eburovices. The Rauraci and Boii each sent two thousand. Thirty thousand total came from the tribes near the Atlantic, commonly called the Armoric Ocean, including the Curiosolities, Redones, Ambibarii, Caletes, Osismi, Veneti, Lemovices, and Venelli. The stubborn Bellovaci, however, sent only a token part of their levied amount to Commius, saying they would fight the Romans on their own terms and that they would obey no one's orders but their own.

Commius had been an ally of Caesar for several years and served him well in Britain. As a reward, Caesar made his tribe exempt from taxes, restored their native laws, and even made the Morini tribe subject to them. But in Gaul at this time there was such a strong desire of liberty and so powerful a yearning to recover their reputation as warriors that no Roman-granted benefits and no memory of past alliances could dissuade them from dedicating their hearts and souls to the war against the Romans. When eight thousand cavalry and about two hundred and fifty thousand infantry had been collected, they met together in the territory of the Aedui. They were all counted and leaders were selected: Commius of the Atrebates, Viridomarus and Eporedorix of the Aedui, and the cousin of Vercingetorix, Vercassivellaunus the Arvernian. A council was selected from all the different tribes and appointed to the leaders to help plan the war. Everyone started out for Alesia boldly full of confidence. Not a single one of them believed anyone could possibly withstand even the sight of such a mighty armed force, especially since the Romans would be facing attacks from the Gauls inside the besieged town as well as the huge army of Gaulish cavalry and infantry outside.

Meanwhile inside the beleaguered town of Alesia, the Gauls had given up hope of relief from their countrymen and had exhausted all their supplies. They had no idea what was going on in the land of the Aedui or that an army was on the way to help them. They called a council of war in Alesia to decide what they should do in these dire circumstances. Some said they should surrender, others said they should make a final attack on the Romans while they still had their strength. But the speech of Critognatus in particular should not be omitted because of his remarkably cruel plan. He was a man of noble birth among the Arvernians and held considerable influence.

"I will not waste one word," he said, "arguing with those who wish to surrender us all to slavery. They have no place as citizens of this land let alone as members of this council. My words are for those who want to attack, for in such daring there is the memory of the warriors we used to be! But I say to you, it is a weakness not to be able to wait for the right time. Among us it is always easier to find those willing to throw themselves into a glorious death in battle than to find those who will patiently wait for the proper moment to attack. I would certainly approve this suicidal plan, so worthy are its proponents, if all we had to lose were our own lives. But we have to consider the rest of Gaul as well, those we have called to our aid. How do you think our brother Gauls will feel when they arrive and have to defeat the Romans standing on our eighty-thousand bodies? Don't rob them of our support when they will have sacrificed so much to help us. Set aside this foolish, reckless, and weak-minded plan which will only deliver Gaul into perpetual slavery. Or do you think help is not coming, just because they're not outside the walls today? Do you really think the Romans are building those walls facing away from our city for their own amusement? Even if we are blocked from receiving messages from the outside, the message of these Romans, laboring day and night out of fear, is crystal clear— help is on the way! What is my plan then? Simple, we do as our ancestors did when the Cimbri and Teutones ravaged our lands. We lock ourselves behind our town walls and sustain ourselves in a similar situation by eating the bodies of those too old or infirm to fight, at least those who have not surrendered themselves to the enemy. Even if we didn't have a precedent for this, I still think it would be a most glorious example of freedom to hand down to our children. But the war with the Cimbri and Teutones was not the same as the present one. For the Cimbri ravaged and destroyed Gaul, but in the end they left our country and sought out other lands, while we preserved our rights, laws, lands, and liberty. But the Romans—what is it they want except to follow their greed, seize the lands of brave men, and reduce them all to eternal slavery? This is how they have conducted every war they have ever fought. And if you don't know what has happened in distant lands across the sea, just look at nearby southern Gaul which they have turned into to a mere province stripped of age-old rights and laws, with its people sold into slavery forever."

When the council had heard everyone's opinion, they decided that anyone who was aged or in poor health should leave the town immediately and that they should try every other option before resorting to the plan of Critognatus. But they determined to follow his plan as a last resort if no Gaulish reinforcements arrived soon rather than surrender to the Romans. The Mandubii, in whose land Alesia lay, were ordered to leave the town along with their wives and children. These came to walls of the Roman camp weeping and begging to be taken in as slaves if only they would be fed, but Caesar posted guards on the wall to send them back.

Finally Commius and the other leaders of the Gauls reached the area of Alesia and seized a hill not more than a mile from the Roman camp. The next day they sent their cavalry out into the plain stretching three miles along the west side of the Roman camp, with the infantry positioned further back on the high ground. The people inside Alesia could look out over the whole plain and were overjoyed at the arrival of reinforcements. The army came out of the town and covered over one of the defensive trenches so that they could be ready to move out and attack the Romans.

Caesar carefully positioned the Roman troops on both walls of the camp, facing both in toward the town and out against the Gaulish army, then he ordered his cavalry out of the camp to attack the Gauls. The Gaulish relief force could look down from their camp on the hill and they were all eagerly awaiting the fight. The Gauls had placed a few archers and light-armed soldiers among their cavalry to offer them relief if they weren't able to resist the charge of the Roman horsemen. A number of Roman soldiers were wounded by these unexpected troops and withdrew back into their camp. The Gauls saw this and grew in confidence that the Romans were losing the battle, with a great cheer and shouting broke out from both those inside the city and those Gauls on the hill. The whole battle was visible and watched by everyone, Gauls and Romans alike, so that no act of bravery or cowardice escaped notice. The desire for praise and the fear of disgrace drove both sides. The fight lasted from noon until sunset, with neither side able to get the upper hand. But then the German auxiliaries of the Romans charged in one part of the field, routing the Gaulish cavalry and surrounding and killing their archers. Then the Roman troops drove the retreating Gauls back to their camp, not giving them any chance to rally their troops and fight back. The Gauls who had come out of Alesia returned to the town in despair at the defeat.

After a day had passed, during which time the Gaulish relief force had made a great number of stick bundles to fill in ditches, scaling ladders, and grappling hooks, the Gauls moved silently out of their camp and made their way to the part of the Roman walls which reached into the plain. They raised a sudden shout as a signal to their besieged comrades inside the town and began to throw down the bundles and used slings, arrows, and stones to dislodge the Romans from their wall. They also did everything else needed for launching an assault. When Vercingetorix had heard the shouts, he signaled his own men with a trumpet and moved out of the town. The Roman soldiers quickly moved each to his assigned station on the wall and began to beat off the Gauls with heavy slings, stakes they had prepared inside the walls, and stones. A great many on both sides received injuries as it was very dark and impossible to see any enemy at a distance—even so the Roman artillery launched a number of volleys. But the legates Marcus Antonius and Gaius Trebonius, who were in charge of that section of the Roman defenses, took no chances and had troops sent to them from other positions along the wall to help their soldiers in the battle.

After two failed attacks, the Gauls were becoming very discouraged and held a council to plan their next step. They decided as a last resort to attack what they perceived as a weak point on a hill in the Roman lines. After a fierce battle, the Romans finally beat back the Gaulish assault and destroyed most of the Gaulish army. Even the bravest of the Gaulish leaders recognized that all hope for Gaulish freedom was now gone (7.89):

On the next day, Vercingetorix called together a council and declared that he had never fought for his own purposes but for the liberty of his whole nation. He then said that as they must now yield to fortune, he would offer himself to the Romans either dead or as a prisoner—so messengers bearing the surrender were sent to Caesar. He ordered all the Gaulish arms handed over and the leaders to be brought forth. Caesar sat in front of the camp while all the weapons were surrendered and the Gaulish leaders were led to him, including Vercingetorix.

Sporadic fighting continued for some time, but the war was effectively over. Vercingetorix was executed in Rome after being forced to march in Caesar's triumphal parade, and all of Gaul was incorporated as a Roman territory for the next four centuries.

* * *

Ammianus Marcellinus wrote at the close of the fourth century A.D. and was the last of the great Roman historians. He describes the Celts of Gaul long after the Roman conquest, but they still show the same martial spirit of earlier days (*History* 15.12.3):

Gauls of all ages are very fit for military service. The old men, made tough by the cold weather and constant physical labor, march forth with courage equal to that of the young, mocking the formidable dangers before them. Nor does anyone cut off his thumb to avoid military duty, as they do in Italy.

FEASTING

Medieval Irish tales speak of loud, rancorous, drunken feasts in which warriors sitting around the main course of a roast pig are as likely as not to end up fighting to the death over some perceived slight or grievance. Classical authors also paint a similar picture of ancient Celtic feasts as rowdy celebrations with an abundance of food and drink—and sometimes with a bloody end as well. Not just the Celts, but many northern peoples were noted by the Greek and Roman writers for their magnificent banquets; but the Celts were known above the rest for the sheer size and exuberant atmosphere of their feasts.

* * *

As early as the fourth century B.C., the Celts were well known for their love of wine. The Greek philosopher Plato has a brief comment on this aspect of the Celtic character in his *Laws*, where he includes the Celts among a list of barbarians who revel in drunkenness (1.637):

I am not discussing the drinking of wine in general, but out-and-out drunkenness. Should we follow the customs of the Scythians and Persians, as well as the Carthaginians, Celts, Iberians, and Thracians, all extremely warlike people, or be like you Spartans who abstain altogether from wine?

* * *

Phylarchus of Athens was one of the most important Greek historians of the third century B.C. His work survives only as fragments quoted by such later authors as Athenaeus, but the passages contain some very interesting information about the dining customs of the Celts which are quite similar to those found two hundred years later in Posidonius. The Celts he refers to may be either Gauls of Europe or Galatians of Asia Minor (Athenaeus *Deipnosophistae* 4.34):

Phylarchus states in his sixth book that among the Celts it is customary to place on the tables many broken loaves along with meat straight from the cauldron. No one eats any of this until they see the king begin to eat his portion.

In his third book Phylarchus says that Ariamnes, a Celt of very great wealth, announced that he would give a year-long feast for all his countrymen, and this is how he accomplished it: He divided the country by marking out convenient distances on the roads. At these points he set up banqueting halls made out of poles, straw, and wicker-work, which each held four hundred men or more, depending on the size of nearby towns and communities. Inside he put huge cauldrons with every kind of meat. The cauldrons were made the year before the feast by artisans from other cities. He then provided many oxen, pigs, sheep, and other kinds of animals every day, along with great jars of wine and an abundance of grain. Not only did the Celts dwelling in nearby towns and villages enjoy the feast, but even strangers passing by were invited in by servants, who urged them to enjoy the good things provided.

* * *

In his book, the *Deipnosophistae* ("Learned Diners"), Athenaeus collects together many stories of dining habits from around the ancient world. His source for the following passages on the Gauls, as he states, is Posidonius (4.151):

Posidonius, using the principles of a Stoic philosopher, describes many different tribes and peoples in his histories. He says that the Celts dine sitting on dry grass in front of wooden tables raised slightly off the ground. They eat small amounts of bread but large quantities of meat, sometimes boiled or roasted and sometimes cooked on spits over an open fire. Like lions, they dine in a surprisingly clean manner, lifting up whole cooked limbs in both hands and taking bites, though they sometimes will cut off a tough portion with a small knife which hangs from their sword sheath in its own covering. Those Celts who live by the sea or along rivers also eat baked fish flavored with salt, vinegar, and the spice cumin. They also use cumin as a flavoring in drinks. They do not use olive oil because it is difficult to obtain, and because of its scarcity it tastes strange to them. Whenever the Celts banquet together they sit in a circle with the most powerful man in the center, like the leader of a Greek chorus. His power may be from bravery in war, noble birth, or wealth. Next to this leader sits the host of the banquet, followed by others of distinction in order of rank on either side. The shield bearers stand behind the diners, while the spearmen are seated in their own circle dining together like their lords. Servers bring drinks in ceramic or even silver cups. The plates are of similar materials, though sometimes they use bronze, woven baskets, or platters made of wood. The wealthy drink wine imported from Italy or the Greek colony of Massalia. This wine is usually, but not always, unwatered. The poorer people drink a type of beer called *corma,* which is sometimes flavored with honey. They pass around a common cup taking small but frequent drinks. The cup is passed to the right, not the left, and by turning to the right in this way they honor their gods.

Posidonius also relates, via Athenaeus, how Gaulish feasts could be a time of heated conflict if tempers got out of control. When Posidonius describes customs prior to his own time, we may be hearing not history but Gaulish mythology, with tales quite similar to those found in early Irish literature (4.154):

In the twenty-third book of his *Histories*, Posidonius says that the Celts sometimes engage in single combat at feasts. These fights begin amiably as a kind of sport with the warriors striking blows at each other in good spirits. But sometimes blood is drawn, tempers rise out of control, and they will fight to the death unless the other guests stop them. Posidonius says that in times past, the bravest man present would claim the choice thigh portion. If anyone challenged him over it, they would fight to the death. Others in the past at feasts would take a pledge of silver, gold, or a certain quantity of wine and distribute it to their friends. This person would stretch himself out face-up on his shield and someone would cut his throat with a sword.

Again drawing primarily on Posidonius, the first-century B.C. Greek writer Diodorus Siculus describes Gaulish eating and drinking habits. His statement that Gaul is too chilly for wine production is true only in certain colder areas, a fact attested by the modern French wine industry. The Gaulish love of imported wine is verified by the many archaeological finds of classical wine jugs in France. Diodorus' description of the lack of restraint among the Gaulish drinkers may be true enough for the most part, but it is also a stereotypical label placed by Greeks on all people beyond the limits of what they considered civilization (*Library* 5.26):

The cold climate of Gaul prevents the growing of grapes for wine or olives for oil. Since the Gauls are deprived of these fruits, they make a drink brewed from barley called *zythos*. They also make a drink from the washings of honeycombs. The Gauls are crazy for wine and consume, unwatered, amazing amounts imported by merchants. Their unrestrained consumption often leads them to fall into a drunken stupor or sink into morose depression. Therefore many Italian merchants see Gaul as the land of opportunity for quick riches. These traders bring the wine by boat on the rivers and by wagon through the plains. In return they make an amazing profit, for they receive a slave in return for each jar of wine they deliver.

Diodorus goes on to describe the appearance of the Gauls and relate more observations on their peculiar dining habits (5.28):

The Gauls are quite tall with fair complexions and rippling muscles. Their hair is not only light by nature, but they use an unusual method to make it even whiter. A lime wash is used frequently as a rinse on their hair, which they then comb back from the forehead all the way to the neck. This makes them look something like Satyrs or Pans with thick horse manes. Some of the common men shave off their facial hair while others wear a short beard. The upper classes shave their cheeks but grow a long moustache which hangs over their mouth. When they drink, the liquid must run through the moustache so that it acts as a sort of strainer. They do not use chairs when they eat but they spread the skins of wolves or dogs on the ground and sit on them. They are served by the youngest of the men and women who have reached maturity. The hearth fires are nearby with both boiling cauldrons and spits of roasting meat. The best men they honor with the choicest portion of meat, just as Homer says Ajax was honored by the Greek kings when he defeated Hector in single combat: "He honored Ajax with slices cut from the whole length of the back." They also invite strangers to their feasts and feed them well before they would dare ask who they are and why they are there. Sometimes at dinner one of them is angered by an offhand remark and will, without any fear for their life, challenge the offender to fight them one-on-one.

As part of the Posidonian tradition, Strabo reports that pork was a favorite Gaulish food—another similarity to medieval Irish tales (*Geography* 4.4.3):

They have large meals with milk and meat of all kinds, but most of all they love pork, both fresh and salted. Their pigs run wild outdoors and are exceptional for their size, speed, and strength.

POETRY

The early Celtic world was a culture in which the deeds of a hero or king survived only in the tales sung around the fire at night by a bard. In our modern world of writing and various other media, it is hard to imagine the power and importance of song and the singer to such a society. The poets of the ancient Celts were literally the voice of their people and, in a society which valued fame and glory, they were the instruments of memory. As in medieval Irish and Welsh society, a poet sang his praise-songs as a professional—he expected to be well paid for his services. Woe be to the king who neglected a bard, as sweet praise could quickly turn to biting satire.

* * *

At the beginning of the first century B.C., a Greek author known as Pseudo-Scymnus records that music, perhaps played by bards, was used at Celtic meetings to calm hot tempers (*Periplus* 186–187):

> With music they conduct their councils,
> using it to soothe the crowd.

* * *

Diodorus Siculus relates the comments of Posidonius on the nature of Gaulish wordplay and use of bombastic language. The Gaulish word *bardos*, which he uses, found its way into English as *bard* (*Library* 5.31):

The Gauls have a fearsome appearance and deep, rough voices. They are a people of few words and often speak in riddles, leaving many things for the listener to understand himself. They love exaggeration both to praise themselves and to belittle others. They are boastful, threatening, and love melodramatic behavior, but they also have sharp minds and are quick learners. They have singing poets called bards who perform playing an instrument like a Greek lyre. These bards sing songs of praise and of satire.

Athenaeus also relays Posidonius' comments on Gaulish poets. The Greek word *parasitos* ("parasite") literally means "dining companion" (*Deipnosophistae* 6.246):

Posidonius of Apameia says in the twenty-third book of his *Histories* that the Celts have with them in war and peace companions whom they call parasites. These men recite the praises of their patrons before gatherings and to all those listening in turn. They are called bards— poets who sing praise.

Posidonius also relates through Athenaeus a wonderful story which illustrates well the relationship between Celtic bard and patron (4.152):

Posidonius tells the story of the wealthy Lovernius son of Bituis, who was removed from power by the Romans. He says that Lovernius rode through the plain on a chariot handing out gold and silver to the thousands of Celts following him in an attempt to win popular support. He also set up a feasting area over a mile square with jars of expensive drink and plentiful food, so that for many days all who wished could enter and enjoy food continuously provided by servants. Lovernius ended the feast on a certain day and was leaving just as one of the Celtic poets arrived. Running beside his chariot, the bard composed a song praising the generosity of Lovernius and bewailing his own late arrival. Lovernius was so delighted by the song that he threw the poet a bag of gold. The tardy poet picked up the bag from behind the chariot and composed another poem, singing that even the tracks of his chariot on the ground yielded benefits to humanity.

* * *

As a young man, the second-century A.D. Greek writer Lucian traveled in Gaul as an itinerant lecturer on literature and philosophy. He records an interesting encounter with a native during his time there which sheds much light on the power and value of the spoken word in ancient Gaul (*Hercules* 1–6):

The Celts call Hercules *Ogmios* in their native language and their representations of him are not at all like our own. In their pictures of him he is a very old man, bald in front with only a few scattered gray hairs in back. His skin is wrinkled and darkly weathered like an ancient sailor. You would think you were looking at a picture of the underworld ferryman Charon or the titan Iapetus buried beneath Hades. But in spite of the way he looks, he has all of Hercules' usual equipment—lion skin on his shoulder, club in his right hand, quiver of arrows at his side, and bow in his left hand—everything you would expect Hercules to possess. I thought at first the Celts were portraying the handsome Hercules like this to spite the Greek gods, since the story goes that Hercules once plundered their country during a cattle-raid while he was chasing the cattle of Geryon through western Europe.

But I haven't yet mentioned the oddest thing of all—the old Hercules of theirs drags behind him a group of men all chained by the ears! The chain is a rare and delicate creation of gold and amber, like the most beautiful of necklaces. Yet although they are bound by such a weak chain and could easily escape if they wanted to, the men following Hercules do not even strain against the chain or resist being led away. They all follow him gladly, pressing close to him and almost stepping on his feet in their effort to stay with him. Apparently they would be deeply offended if they were released. But the strangest thing is where the painter attached the chain to Hercules. Since his hands already were full with the club and the bow, the chain was fixed to the tip of his tongue as he turns towards his captives and smiles.

I stood for a long time looking at this picture, full of puzzlement, anger, and wonder, until a Celt standing near me spoke. He was well-educated in our ways, as shown by his excellent Greek, and familiar with the local traditions: "I can explain the riddle of the picture to you, stranger, since you seem confused and disturbed by it. We Celts do not agree with you Greeks that Hermes represents eloquence. We think instead that the power of the spoken word is best shown by Hercules, since he is much stronger. And don't be surprised that we portray him as an old man. Eloquence is most likely to reveal itself in the fullness of age, not in youth. As your poets themselves say, 'The mind of a young man wanders' and 'Old age speaks more wisely than youth.' That is why the old man Nestor's words are like honey and the words of the old Trojan men are like flowers—lilies, if I remember my Homer. So if you see old Hercules here leading men away by his tongue, don't be surprised. You should know the kinship between tongue and ear. And it is no insult that his tongue is pierced, for as I remember a comic poet of your own country said, 'All those who talk much have tongues pierced at the tip.' Our common tradition is that Hercules achieved most of his great deeds by using the power of words. I suppose the arrows in his quiver represent words—sharp, fast, and hitting the target—which pierce the spirit of the listener. You Greeks yourselves do say that words have wings."

And that is what the Celt told me.

* * *

In the late fourth century A.D., Ammianus Marcellinus briefly describes the Gaulish bards of old as poets much like the Greek Homer (*History* 15.9.8):

And the bards sang the great deeds of famous men in heroic verse, accompanied by the sweet tones of the lyre.

RELIGION

orks discussing ancient Celtic religion very often begin and end with the Druids, the Celtic priestly class. But while the Druids were certainly an important part of Celtic religious beliefs, they were not the whole story. Ancient writers tell of a variety of religious customs and practices of the Celts, including many forms of prophecy and magic which don't seem to have involved the Druids at all. And when we do look at the surviving sources on the Druids, we may be sadly disappointed at just how little we really know about this group. What we do know may be surprising, such as the fact that of the few individual Druids known from antiquity, some are women. Druids may or may not have been found throughout the ancient Celtic lands—we have no record of them in Celtic Spain or Galatia for example—but our sources are not complete. Our knowledge of ancient Celtic religion in general is very sparse and of course we must keep in mind that we are dealing with a geographically diverse and nonhomogeneous group of tribes over a period of many centuries.

* * *

The earliest reference we have to Celtic religion introduces the theme of human sacrifice found in a number of later authors. The writer is the late fourth-century B.C. playwright Sopater, who, in a fragmentary passage found in Athenaeus, rails against counterfeit philosophers in a comic tirade. Although the passage is humorous, he expects his audience to appreciate the reference to a Celtic ritual which must have been viewed by them as very real (*Deipnosophistae* 4.160):

Among them is the custom,
whenever they are victorious in battle,
to sacrifice their prisoners to the gods.
So I, like the Celts, have vowed to the divine powers
to burn those three false dialecticians as an offering.

* * *

The early third-century Greek historian Timaeus from Sicily provides the earliest information about particular Celtic gods in one of his surviving fragments. It may surprise us that these gods are none other than the twins Castor and Pollux, popular Greek divinities who are sons of Zeus and known as the Dioscori. But the practice of giving foreign gods classical names is standard in ancient writing and reveals only that the unfamiliar gods seemed similar in some way to the Greek or Roman gods better known by the writer (Diodorus Siculus *Geography* 4.56):

Historians point out that the Celts who live on the shore of the Ocean honor the Dioscori above other gods. For there is an ancient tradition among them that these gods came to them from the Ocean.

What we can infer about Celtic religion from this passage is that some Celtic tribe bordering the Atlantic Ocean, probably in Gaul, worshiped twin gods as their chief deities and preserved an old tradition that these gods had once come to them from the sea.

* * *

A fragment of the late third-century B.C. historian Eudoxus of Rhodes, found in the second-century A.D. writer Aelian, relates a story of early Celtic animal magic (*On Animals* 17.19):

Eudoxus says that the Celts do the following (and if anyone thinks his account credible, let him believe it; if not, let him ignore it). When clouds of locusts invade their country and damage the crops, the Celts evoke certain prayers and offer sacrifices which charm birds—and the birds hear these prayers, come in flocks, and destroy the locusts. If however one of them should capture one of these birds, his punishment according to the laws of the country is death. If he is pardoned and released, this throws the birds into a rage, and to revenge the captured bird they do not respond if they are called on again.

* * *

The historian Livy, drawing on early sources, records the death of the Roman general Postumius in 216 B.C. at the hands of Cisalpine Gauls in northern Italy. The custom of using a skull as a sacred vessel is also found among other ancient peoples, such as the Scythians of the Russian steppe (*From the Founding of the City* 23.24):

Postumius died there fighting with all his might not to be captured alive. The Gauls stripped him of all his spoils and the Boii took his severed head in a procession to the holiest of their temples. There it was cleaned and the bare skull was adorned with gold, as is their custom. It was used thereafter as a sacred vessel on special occasions and as a ritual drinking-cup by their priests and temple officials.

* * *

Nicander of Colophon in Asia Minor was a Hellenistic poet who probably lived in the second century B.C. One surviving fragment of Nicander is found in the early Christian theologian Tertullian (*De anima* 57.10):

It is often said because of visions in dreams that the dead truly live. The Nasamones receive special oracles by staying at the tombs of their parents, as Heraclides — or Nymphodorus or Herodotus — writes. The Celts also for the same reason spend the night near the tombs of their famous men, as Nicander affirms.

Tertullian's purpose in writing *De anima* was to combat pagan philosophical ideas concerning the soul and to argue for his own Christian beliefs. He presents the Nasamones tribe of Libya and the Celts as two misguided cultures believing in the reality of visions from the dead. This is our earliest reference to

Celtic beliefs about life after death. Celtic ideas about an afterlife as found in later Irish and Welsh literature are an ambiguous mixture of reincarnation and an otherworldly Land of the Dead. The idea of grave-mounds as gateways to the Otherworld, however, is a common theme in both later Irish and Welsh literature, as when the ancient Irish hero Fergus mac Roich rises from his tomb to recount the lost story of the *Táin Bó Cúailnge*. Nicander's passage shows that the cultural basis for otherworldly contact was present in Celtic mythology and religious practice at least as early as the second century B.C.

* * *

The late second-century B.C. geographer Artemidorus of Ephesus was a Greek who had traveled as far as the Atlantic shores of Spain and perhaps Gaul. His works were often quoted by later authors. In one passage, he relates a story of a ritual involving birds, as in the passage of Eudoxus above, but in this case the birds are used to decide a dispute rather than as protection for crops. Strabo, often a skeptic, reports the ritual in his *Geography* (4.4.6):

The following story which Artemidorus has told about the crows is unbelievable. There is a certain harbor on the coast which, according to him, is named "Two Crows." In this harbor are seen two crows, with their right wings somewhat white. Men who are in dispute about certain matters come here, put a plank on an elevated place, and then each man separately throws up cakes of barley. The birds fly up and eat some of the cakes, but scatter others. The man whose cakes are scattered wins the dispute. Although this story is implausible, his report about the goddesses Demeter and Core is more credible. He says that there is an island near Britain on which sacrifices are performed like those in Samothrace for Demeter and Core.

Birds were frequently part of divination rituals throughout the ancient world, as they were seen as intermediaries between the gods above and people below. The location of this harbor in the

Celtic lands is unknown and could be anywhere from Mediterranean Spain to the Atlantic coast of Gaul. The "island near Britain" is also unnamed, but could possibly be one of the small islands off the coast of France or even Ireland. Demeter and Core (also known as Persephone) were worshipped throughout the Greek world in harvest and fertility festivals and in rituals involving the cycle of the seasons.

* * *

Posidonius (via Diodorus Siculus) relates a number of religious customs in Gaul at the beginning of the first century B.C., several decades before the Roman conquest. These include the establishment of inviolate sacred places for dedications of goods to the gods, a custom also found among the Greeks and Romans (*Library* 5.27):

The Celts of the Gaulish interior have their own custom which is otherwise contradictory to their nature. They have sanctuaries of their the gods throughout the country at which they dedicate large amounts of gold to their divinities. Because of the sacred nature of these places, no one would dare to touch this gold, even though the Celts are great lovers of money.

Diodorus also reports on the Gaulish belief in reincarnation, similar to that of the Greek philosopher Pythagoras (5.28):

The teaching of Pythagoras prevails among the Gauls, that the souls of humans are immortal and that after a certain number of years they will live again, with the soul passing into another body. Because of this belief, some people at funerals will throw letters into the funeral pyre, so that those having passed on might read them.

Note that this doctrine of reincarnation is not one of immediate rebirth, but reincorporation of the spirit into a new body after an undefined length of time. Where the souls not yet reborn exist is unstated, but relatives believed they could send letters to dead loved-ones through the portal apparently opened at a funeral pyre.

Through Diodorus, Posidonius also details a particularly gruesome religious rite of the Gauls and comments on the power of their religious officials (5.31):

The Gauls have certain wise men and experts on the gods called Druids, as well as a highly respected class of seers. Through auguries and animal sacrifice these seers predict the future and no one dares to scoff at them. They have an especially odd and unbelievable method of divination for the most important matters. Having anointed a human victim, they stab him with a small knife in the area above the diaphragm. When the man has collapsed from the wound, they interpret the future by observing the nature of his fall, the convulsion of his limbs, and especially from the pattern of his spurting blood. In this type of divination, the seers place great trust in an ancient tradition of observation.

It is a custom among the Gauls to never perform a sacrifice without someone skilled in divine ways present. They say that those who know about the nature of the gods should offer thanks to them and make requests of them, as though these people spoke the same language as the gods. The Gauls, friends and foes alike, obey the rule of the priests and bards not only in time of peace but also during wars. It has often happened that just as two armies approached each other with swords drawn and spears ready, the Druids will step between the two sides and stop the fighting, as if they had cast a spell on wild beasts. Thus even among the wildest barbarians, anger yields to wisdom and the god of war respects the Muses.

Diodorus also relates other types of human sacrifice among the Gauls (5.32):

It is in keeping with their wildness and savage nature that they carry out particularly offensive religious practices. They will keep some criminal under guard for five years, then impale him on a pole in honor of their gods—followed by burning him on an enormous pyre along with many other first-fruits. They also use prisoners of war as sacrifices to the gods. Some of the Gauls will even sacrifice animals captured in war, either by slaying them, burning them, or by killing them with some other type of torture.

The first of these painful rituals suggests that it was done as part of a harvest festival held every five years, with the first fruits of the land offered to the gods along with the condemned man. The lack of uniformity in sacrificing captured animals is also worth noting—evidence that Gaulish religious customs varied by tribe.

Strabo carries on the Posidonian tradition with several passages on Gaulish religious life (*Geography* 4.4.4–5):

Generally speaking, there are three uniquely honored groups among the Gauls: Bards, Vates, and Druids. The Bards are singers and poets, while the Vates oversee sacred rites and examine natural phenomena. The Druids also study the ways of nature, but apply themselves to laws of morality as well. The Gauls consider the Druids the most just of people and so are entrusted with judging both public and private disputes. In the past, they even stopped battles which were about to begin and brought an end to wars. Murder cases especially are handed over to the Druids for judgment. They believe that when there are many condemned criminals available for sacrifice, then the land will prosper. Both the Druids and others say that the human soul and the universe as well are indestructible, but that at some time both fire and water will prevail.

The Romans have put a stop to the display of severed heads in Gaulish homes, as well as sacrificial and divination customs opposed to our civilized way of life.

Strabo also passes on one of the most interesting reports of Gaulish religious life. A cult of women is compared to worshippers of Dionysus, Greek god of wine, but the practices are certainly Celtic in origin (4.4.6):

Posidonius also says there is a small island in the Atlantic Ocean at the mouth of the Loire River inhabited by women of the Samnitae tribe. They are possessed by Dionysus and appease this god by mysterious ceremonies and other types of sacred rituals. No man ever comes to this island, but the women sail to the mainland to have sex with men, then return. Each year the women take down the roof of a temple and build it again before dark, with each woman carrying a load to add to the roof. Whoever drops her load is torn to pieces by the others. They then carry the pieces of her around the temple shouting with a Bacchanalian cry until their mad frenzy passes away. And it always happens that the one who is going to suffer this fate is bumped by someone.

Finally, Strabo briefly notes the Gaulish custom of depositing rich offerings to the gods in bodies of water, as well as in temples (4.1.13):

Posidonius and many others have noted that as Gaul was both rich in gold and the people very devoted to the gods, there were many places which had stores of treasure. The people would often place these heavy offerings of silver and gold in lakes as they were the safest locations. The Romans auctioned off these lakes for their public treasury once they had conquered a region and the buyers often found millstones of hammered silver in them. At Tolosa in southern Gaul there was also a very sacred temple honored by the people of that area. It was full of sacred treasure dedicated by numerous people and no one would think of ever touching what it contained.

* * *

Caesar is one of our best classical sources on the Druids. He provides a full description of Gaulish religious life as an aside to the description of his war against the Gauls. Certainly some of his information comes from Posidonius (note the similarities to the previous passages of Diodorus and Strabo), but Caesar had enough firsthand contact with the Gauls as both allies and enemies to provide a valuable account of the Druids and religion in Gaulish society and also to relate important information on Gallic social structure in general (*Gallic War* 6.13–14, 16):

Throughout all of Gaul there are two classes of people who are treated with dignity and honor. This does not include the common people, who are little better than slaves and never have a voice in councils. Many of these align themselves with a patron voluntarily, whether because of debt or heavy tribute or out of fear of retribution by some other powerful person. Once they do this, they have given up all rights and are scarcely better than servants. The two powerful classes mentioned above are the Druids and the warriors. Druids are concerned with religious matters, public and private sacrifices, and divination.

A great many young men come to the Druids for instruction, holding them in great respect. Indeed, the Druids are the judges on all controversies public and private. If any crime has been committed, if any murder done, if there are any questions concerning inheritance, or any controversy concerning boundaries, the Druids decide the case and determine punishments. If anyone ignores their decision, that person is banned from all sacrifices—an extremely harsh punishment among the Gauls. Those who are so condemned are considered detestable criminals. Everyone shuns them and will not speak with them, fearing some harm from contact with them, and they receive no justice nor honor for any worthy deed.

Among all the Druids there is one who is the supreme leader, holding highest authority over the rest. When the chief Druid dies, whoever is the most worthy succeeds him. If there are several of equal standing, a vote of all the Druids follows, though the leadership is sometimes contested even by armed force. At a certain time of the year, all the Druids gather together at a consecrated spot in the territory of the Carnutes, whose land is held to be the center of all Gaul. Everyone gathers there from the whole land to present disputes and they obey the judgments and decrees of the Druids. It is said that the druidic movement began in Britain and was then carried across to Gaul. Even today, those who wish to study their teachings most diligently usually travel to Britain.

The Druids are exempt from serving in combat and from paying war taxes, unlike all other Gauls. Tempted by such advantages, many young people willingly commit themselves to druidic studies while others are sent by their parents. It is said that in the schools of the Druids they learn a great number of verses, so many in fact that some students spend twenty years in training. It is not permitted to write down any of these sacred teachings, though other public and private transactions are often recorded in Greek letters. I believe they practice this oral tradition for two reasons: first, so that the common crowd does not gain access to their secrets and second, to improve the faculty of memory. Truly, writing does often weaken one's diligence in learning and reduces the ability to memorize. The cardinal teaching of the Druids is that the soul does not perish, but after death passes from one body to another. Because of this teaching that death is only a transition, they are able to encourage fearlessness in battle. They have a great many other teachings as well which they hand down to the young concerning such things as the motion of the stars, the size of the cosmos and the earth, the order of the natural world, and the power of the immortal gods.

All of the Gauls are greatly devoted to religion, and because of this those who are afflicted with terrible illnesses or face dangers in battle will conduct human sacrifices, or at least vow to do so. The Druids are the ministers at such occasions. They believe that unless the life of a person is offered for the life of another, the dignity of the immortal gods will be insulted. This is true both in private and public sacrifices. Some build enormous figures which they fill with living persons and then set on fire, everyone perishing in flames. They believe that the execution of thieves and other criminals is the most pleasing to the gods, but, when the supply of guilty persons runs short, they will kill the innocent as well.

Caesar next discusses the individual gods of the Gauls. Not surprisingly, given his own background and that of his readers, he describes them in Roman terms using Roman names (6.17–18):

The chief god of the Gauls is Mercury and there are images of him everywhere. He is said to be the inventor of all the arts, the guide for every road and journey, and the most influential god in trade and moneymaking. After him, they worship Apollo, Mars, Jupiter, and Minerva. These gods have the same areas of influence as among most other peoples. Apollo drives away diseases, Minerva is most influential in crafts, Jupiter rules the sky, and Mars is the god of war. Before a great battle, they will often dedicate the spoils to Mars. If they are successful, they will sacrifice all the living things they have captured and other spoils they gather together in one place. Among many tribes, you can see these spoils placed together in a sacred spot. And it is a very rare occasion that anyone would dare to disturb these valuable goods and conceal them in his home. If it does happen, the perpetrator is tortured and punished in the worst ways imaginable.

The Gauls all say that they are descended from the god of the dark underworld, Dis, and confirm that this is the teaching of the Druids. Because of this they measure time by the passing of nights, not days. Birthdays and the beginnings of months and years all start at night.

Caesar's Mercury is likely to be the pan-Celtic god *Lugus*, known from Gaulish and Celtiberian inscriptions. He appears in many ancient Celtic place names, such as *Lugudunum* ("the fort of Lugus"), modern Lyon in France. In medieval Irish sources he appears as *Lug*, a divine figure of many skills and god of the annual Lughnasadh festival still celebrated on August 1st. In Welsh tales he survives as the skilled shoemaker *Lleu*.

Caesar also confirms the Gaulish practice of grand funerals and human sacrifice, at least in former times, as a part of these rituals (6.19):

The funerals of the Gauls are magnificent and extravagant. Everything which was dear to the departed is thrown into the fire, including animals. In the recent past, they would also burn faithful slaves and beloved subordinates at the climax of the funeral.

* * *

The first-century B.C. Roman orator Cicero records his personal experiences with a Druid in a treatise addressed to his brother Quintus (*On Divination* 1.90):

The practice of divination is not even neglected by barbarians. I know there are Druids in Gaul because I met one myself—Divitiacus of the Aedui tribe, who was your guest and praised you highly. He claimed a knowledge of nature derived from what the Greeks call "physiologia"—the inquiry into natural causes and phenomena. He would predict the future using augury and other forms of interpretation.

* * *

The Celts did not uniformly follow traditional religious practices. Often, because of political or personal reasons, they would
embrace new ways. One example is the accession to the priest-
hood of the imperial cult of the divine Augustus by certain Galatian nobles in the early first century A.D. But such a move was
largely political and did not preclude other forms of worship.
An inscription records the names of Galatian priests over two
generations and their contributions to the temple (*Orientis
Graeci Inscriptiones Selectae* 533):

Albiorix son of Ateporix gave two public feasts (A.D. 23/24, 26/27)

Aristocles son of Albiorix gave a public feast (A.D. 34/35)

* * *

The encyclopedic *Natural History* of the Roman author Pliny
was published just two years before he perished in the eruption
of Vesuvius in A.D. 79. In it we have several detailed accounts of
druidic rituals and a general description of Celtic religion in
the century after the Roman conquest of Gaul (16.249, 24.103–
104, 29.52, 30.13):

I can't forget to mention the admiration the Gauls have for mistletoe.
The Druids (which is the name of their holy men) hold nothing more
sacred than this plant and the tree on which it grows—as if it grew
only on oaks. They worship only in oak groves and will perform no
sacred rites unless a branch of that tree is present. It seems the Druids
even get their name from *drus* (the Greek word for oak). And indeed
they think that anything which grows on an oak tree is sent from
above and is a sign that the tree was selected by the god himself. The
problem is that in fact mistletoe rarely grows on oak trees. Still they
search it out with great diligence and then will cut it only on the sixth
day of the moon's cycle, because the moon is then growing in power
but is not yet halfway through its course (they use the moon to measure not only months but years and their grand cycle of thirty years).
In their language they call mistletoe a name meaning "all-healing."
They hold sacrifices and sacred meals under oak trees, first leading
forward two white bulls with horns bound for the first time. A priest

44

dressed in white then climbs the tree and cuts the mistletoe with a golden sickle, with the plant dropping onto a white cloak. They then sacrifice the bulls while praying that the god will favorably grant his own gift to those to whom he has given it. They believe a drink made with mistletoe will restore fertility to barren livestock and act as a remedy to all poisons. Such is the devotion to frivolous affairs shown by many peoples.

Similar to the Sabine herb savin is a plant called *selago*. It must be picked without an iron instrument by passing the right hand through the opening of the left sleeve, as if you were stealing it. The harvester, having first offered bread and wine, must wear white and have clean, bare feet. It is carried in a new piece of cloth. The Druids of Gaul say that it should be used to ward off every danger and that the smoke of burning selago is good for eye diseases. The Druids also gather a plant from marshes called *samolus*, which must be picked with the left hand during a time of fasting. It is good for the diseases of cows, but the one who gathers it must not look back nor place it anywhere except in the watering trough of the animals.

There is a kind of egg which is very famous in Gaul but ignored by Greek writers. In the summer months, a vast number of snakes will gather themselves together in a ball which is held together by their saliva and a secretion from their bodies. The Druids say they produce this egg-like object called an *anguinum* which the hissing snakes throw up into the air. It must be caught, so they say, in a cloak before it hits the ground. But you'd better have a horse handy, because the snakes will chase you until they are cut off by some stream. A genuine anguinum will float upstream, even if covered in gold. But as is common with the world's holy men, the Druids say it can only be gathered during a particular phase of the moon, as if people could make the moon and serpents work together. I saw one of these eggs myself—it was a small round thing like an apple with a hard surface full of indentations as on the arms of an octopus. The Druids value them highly. They say it is a great help in lawsuits and will help you gain the good will of a ruler. That this is plainly false is shown by a man of the Gaulish Vocontii tribe, a Roman knight, who kept one hidden in his cloak during a trial before the emperor Claudius and was executed, as far as I can tell, for this reason alone.

Barbarous rites were found in Gaul even within my own memory. For it was then that the emperor Tiberius passed a decree through the senate outlawing their Druids and these types of diviners and physicians. But why do I mention this about a practice which has crossed the sea and reached the ends of the earth? For even today Britain performs rites with such ceremony that you would think they were the source for the extravagant Persians. It is amazing how distant people are so similar in such practices. But at least we can be glad that the Romans have wiped out the murderous cult of the Druids, who thought human sacrifice and ritual cannibalism were the greatest kind of piety.

* * *

The Roman biographer Suetonius states that the Emperor Claudius, who ruled A.D. 41–54, continued the policy against the Druids initiated earlier by Tiberius (*Claudius* 25):

Claudius destroyed the horrible and inhuman religion of the Gaulish Druids, which had merely been forbidden to Roman citizens under Augustus.

* * *

The Roman geographer Pomponius Mela wrote a description of the world during the reign of Claudius. Much of his information is taken from Caesar, but he does provide a few new details on the Druids, such as their adaptations to Roman rule (*De chorographia* 3.18–19):

The horrible practices of the Gauls have been abolished, yet some of their customs still linger on. Though they no longer slaughter human victims, they still require a little blood from them on the way to make a sacrifice. The Gauls do have a kind of eloquence, however, and teachers of wisdom called Druids. These men claim to know the size and shape of the earth and universe, the motion of the stars and the sky, and the will of the gods. They teach many things secretly to the Gaulish nobles over a period of up to twenty years in caves and hidden places in the forest.

* * *

In the first century A.D., the Latin poet Lucan gives us the name of three Gaulish gods. His description is brief, unflattering, and full of poetic flourish, but undoubtedly reflects a genuine tradition (*Civil War* 1.444–446):

> Cruel Teutates pleased by dreadful blood,
> Horrid Esus with his barbaric altars,
> and Taranis, more cruel than Scythian Diana.

Later classical commentaries on this passage claim that victims of Teutates were drowned by plunging them headfirst into a cauldron, those of Esus were hung from trees, and sacrifices to Taranis were burned in wooden cages.

Lucan continues with a poetic description of the Druids (1.450–458):

> Oh Druids, now that the war is over
> you return to your barbaric rites and sinister ways.
> You alone know the ways of the gods and powers of heaven,
> or perhaps you don't know at all.
> You who dwell in dark and remote forest groves,
> you say that the dead do not seek the silent realm of Erebus
> or the pale kingdom of Pluto,
> but that the same spirit lives again in another world
> and death, if your songs are true, is but the middle of a long life.

* * *

We know very little about the religion of the Celtiberians of Spain (ancient Iberia or Hiberia), but the first-century A.D. Roman poet Silius Italicus does relate one interesting aspect of their culture (*Punica* 3.340–343):

> The Celts known as Hiberi came also.
> To them it is glorious to fall in combat,
> but they consider it wrong to cremate a warrior
> who dies in this way.

They believe he will be carried up to the gods
if his body, lying on the field of battle,
is devoured by a hungry vulture.

* * *

The Greek travel writer Pausanius about A.D. 150 relates an interesting taboo of the Tolistobogii tribe of Galatia concerning the eating of pigs—a prohibition which distinguishes them sharply from the pork-loving Gauls of western Europe (*Description of Greece* 17.10):

The Galatians who live around the city of Pessinus will not consume pork.

Pausanius claims this is due to a local legend about the Asiatic god Attis being killed by a wild boar.

* * *

Lucian in the second century A.D. records that Galatians sought out the foreign soothsayer Alexander in nearby Paphlagonia (*Alexander* 51):

Alexander often gave prophesies to non-Greeks. And if anyone asked a question in his native language, Syrian or Celtic, he easily found interpreters in the city of the same origin as the questioners.

* * *

An inscription from A.D. 166 found in Galatia states that the Celtic Nobantenoi tribe had not abandoned their traditional worship (in spite of the influence of Christianity), but whether this religion was Celtic, Greek, or a mixed form is unknown (*Regional Epigraphic Catalogues of Asia Minor* 11.75):

From ancestral times, the Nobantenoi have sacrificed to Zeus according to their custom.

* * *

It is important to note that Christianity reached Gaul (as well as Britain) at an early point and prospered among the Celts there, competing with native Celtic beliefs and Roman religious practices. The Greek bishop and theologian Irenaeus preached in the late second century at Lyons. Not one to suffer in silence, he complained about having to learn Gaulish to serve his flock (*Against Heresies* 1, preface):

You must pardon the lack of elegance from those of us who live among the Celts, for we are accustomed to translate our words constantly into a barbarous language.

* * *

The fourth-century A.D. collection of imperial biographies known as the *Historia Augusta* contains three short passages involving Gaulish women called *Dryades* ("Druidesses"). The first refers to the emperor Alexander Severus in A.D. 235 when he was setting off to drive the Germans from Gaul (Lampridius *Alexander Severus* 59.5):

The Druidess exclaimed to him as he went, "Go ahead, but don't hope for victory or put any trust in your soldiers."

A few decades later, the future emperor Diocletian encountered a Druidess. Years later, he became emperor after killing the imperial assassin Aper ("the Boar") (Vopiscus *Numerianus* 14):

While Diocletian was still a young soldier he was staying at a tavern in the land of the Tongri in Gaul. Every day he had to settle his account with the landlady, a Druidess. One day she said, "Diocletian, you are greedy and cheap!" Jokingly he responded to her, "Then I'll be more generous when I'm emperor." "Don't laugh," she said, "for you'll be emperor after you've killed the boar."

The final passage speaks of the emperor Aurelian, who ruled for five years beginning in A.D. 270 (Vopiscus *Aurelianus* 43.4):

On certain occasions Aurelian would consult Gaulish Druidesses to discover whether or not his descendants would continue to rule. They told him that no name would be more famous than those of the line of Claudius. And indeed, the current emperor Constantius is a descendant of his.

In all of these, the women may not be direct heirs of the Druids who were supposedly wiped out by the Romans—but in any case they do show that the druidic function of prophesy continued among the natives in Roman Gaul.

* * *

Ammianus Marcellinus in the late fourth century A.D. draws on earlier sources in his description of the Druids (whom he calls *Drysidae*) and their companion *Euhages* (otherwise known as *Vates*). His Euhages seem to be concerned with natural science, whereas the Druids prefer history and speculative philosophy (*History* 15.9.4, 8):

The Drysidae claim that a part of the Gaul's population was indigenous, but that others arrived from distant islands and lands to the east of the Rhine River, driven from their homelands by frequent wars and floods of the stormy sea.

Throughout the regions of Gaul the tribes slowly became more civilized and began to study praiseworthy doctrines initiated by the Bards, Euhages, and Drysidae . . . The Euhages investigated the sublime secrets of the universe, seeking to understand the hidden laws of nature. The Drysidae were the most intelligent of all and bound themselves into a secret brotherhood, as the rule of Pythagoras dictates. They rose above the rest by their study of the obscure and sublime, and despising things merely human, declared that the soul is immortal.

* * *

The Latin poet Ausonius lived and taught in Gaul in the late fourth century A.D., rising to a position of great power in the Roman government. Two brief passages in his collection of poems addressed to fellow professors show that the memory of the Druids lived on at the end of the Roman Empire and druidic ancestry could even be a point of pride (*Commemoratio* 4.7–10, 10.22–30):

> You are descended from the Druids of Bayeux,
> if the stories about you are true,
> and you trace your sacred ancestry and renown
> from the temple of Belenus.
>
> Nor will I forget the old man
> by the name of Phoebicius.
> Though he was priest of the god Belenus,
> he received no profit from the position.
> But nonetheless this one,
> who descended, it is said,
> from the Druids of Brittany,
> did receive a professorship at Bordeaux
> with the help of his son.

WOMEN

Ancient Celtic women are sometimes portrayed in modern stories as enjoying complete independence and equal rights within their societies—a romantic view not supported in the classical sources. A Celtic wife was completely subject to her husband's will just as a Roman matron lived under the rule of her husband as *pater familias*. On the other hand, women of the Celts did generally enjoy more freedom and opportunity than their counterparts in the Greek and Roman world. It is hard to imagine a Greek wife joining her husband on the battlefield or even leading an army, as did the British queen Boudicca. Still, the limited information we have on the lives of Celtic women shows that it was above all a man's world.

* * *

Athenaeus reports a story supposedly found in the now-lost *Constitution of Massalia* of Aristotle. Massalia (modern Marseilles on the southern coast of France) was founded *c.* 600 B.C. by Phocaean Greek colonists in the land of the Celtic Segobrigii tribe. Although the story has many mythological elements, it is a fitting introduction to strong-willed Celtic women who often follow their own path (*Deipnosophistae* 13.576):

The people of Phocaea were devoted to trade and thus founded the colony of Massalia. Euxenos of Phocaea was a guest of the native king in that area who was named Nannos. By chance, Nannos was celebrating the wedding of his daughter when Euxenos arrived and he was invited to attend the ceremonies. The wedding custom among them was that after dinner the young woman was to mix a cup of wine and present it to one of the suitors who was present. Whoever she gave it to would be her husband. When the time came, the daughter gave the cup to Euxenos, perhaps by accident or perhaps by choice (the name of the bride was Petta). When this happened, the father believed it was a sign from the gods and so gave his daughter to Euxenos. The Greek took her for his wife and changed her name to Aristoxene. Even today there is a family in Massalia called the Protiadai, named after Protis, the son of Euxenos and Aristoxene.

The mythological nature of the story is clearly shown in the names of the characters. The Greek *Euxenos* means "good foreigner" while the second name of Petta is Greek *Aristoxene*, "the best foreign woman." *Petta* itself seems to be a Celtic term meaning "portion" or "share" (compare Welsh *peth* "portion, thing"), suggesting that Petta represents the portion of land the Greeks were seeking. The son's name, *Protis*, simply means "the first."

* * *

A collection of short Greek poems from the fourth century B.C. onwards, the *Greek Anthology* took shape over a number of centuries at the hands of various editors. One of the epigrams of the collection by an anonymous poet includes an interesting account of paternity testing among the Gauls. The account is surely rich in poetic license, but there may be a genuine ritual behind the verse. Over a century later, Caesar affirms that Gaulish men had the power of life and death over their wives and children (*Greek Anthology* 9.125):

> The bold Celts test their children in the jealous Rhine
> and no man regards himself as a true father
> until he sees the child washed in the holy river.
> For immediately when the child has come from
> the mother's womb and shed its first tears, the father picks
> it up and places it on his own shield, not sympathizing,
> for he does not feel for the child like a true father
> until he sees it judged in the river's bath.
> And the mother, having new pains added to those
> of childbirth, even if she knows him to be the true father,
> awaits in fear what the inconstant river will judge.

The exact method of testing is not mentioned here, but centuries later the Emperor Julian notes that illegitimate Gaulish newborns supposedly sink in the waters of the Rhine (*Epistle* 59).

* * *

The Greek biographer Plutarch relates a story drawn from the late second-century B.C. historian Polybius concerning a remarkable Galatian named Chiomara, a woman of high rank who lived during the Roman subjugation of Galatia in the early second century B.C. (*The Virtuous Deeds of Women* 22):

Chiomara, the wife of Ortiagon, was captured along with the other Galatian women when the Romans under Gnaeus Manlius conquered the Asiatic Galatians. The centurion responsible for her took advantage of his soldierly power and raped her. This man was an ignorant beast who loved both pleasure and money, but in the end his love of money won out. With a large ransom having been agreed on, he led her to a certain river across from agents of her own people. The Galatians crossed over and gave him the money, but after they did so, Chiomara signaled them to strike down the centurion as he was making a friendly farewell. One of her countrymen obeyed and cut off his head. She took the head, wrapped it in her cloak, and went home. When she returned to her husband, she threw the head down at his feet. Ortiagon was amazed and said, "My wife, it is important to deal honorably." "Yes," she said, "but it is more important that only one man who has slept with me should remain alive." Polybius says he met and conversed with Chiomara later in Sardis and that he was struck by her intelligence and indomitable spirit.

Plutarch also tells the story of the Galatian priestess and queen Camma (*The Virtuous Deeds of Women* 20):

In Galatia, the two most powerful rulers were Sinatus and Sinorix, distant relatives of each other. Sinatus had married a woman named Camma who was admired for her beauty and kindness, but even more so for her virtue. She was also modest and generous, showing great kindness to the common people because of her wonderful qualities. In addition, she was well known as a priestess of the goddess Artemis, who the Galatians worship most of all. She was always exquisitely dressed in the fine robes of her office during processions and religious ceremonies.

Sinorix fell in love with her, but was not able to seduce her by persuasion or force. Finally he committed an awful deed and treacherously killed her husband. He quickly began a courtship of Camma, who was then spending most of her time in the temple of Artemis. She wasn't weeping or wailing, but bore herself sensibly as one who was biding her time. Every day he attempted to persuade her to marry him. He was full of arguments which seemed reasonable enough— that he was in every way a better man than Sinatus and that he had only killed him out of his passionate desire to be with Camma. At first she rebuffed him with only mild bitterness, but he seemed to be slowly making headway with her. Her family and friends, trying to win favor with Sinatus as he was a powerful man, also began to put pressure on her to marry him. Finally she gave in and sent a message to him that she would have him if the marriage would take place in the temple of the goddess. He gladly consented and she warmly welcomed him when he arrived, leading him to the altar. She poured a ritual drink into a libation bowl and drank of it, asking that he then drink as well—but it was in fact a poisoned mixture of milk and honey (a drink offered to the gods of the underworld). When she saw that he had drunk it, she cried with joy and threw herself down before the image of the goddess. "I call on you, most revered goddess," she said, "to witness that I have lived only for this day of vengeance. For the sake of my murdered husband Sinatus I have endured the days, hoping only for justice. As justice has now come, I go now to join my husband. But you Sinorix, most evil of men, tell your family to prepare a tomb for you instead of a marriage bed."

As Sinorix heard these words, he began to feel the poison working its way through his body. He jumped into his chariot to try to shake and jolt himself into throwing up the poison, but he rapidly became weak and was carried off to bed. He died that evening, but Camma lasted through the night. When she at last heard of Sinorix's death, she died herself, happy and at peace.

* * *

Posidonius, via Diodorus Siculus, describes the abundance of gold jewelry worn by both women and men, a common find in archaeological excavations of Celtic tombs (*Library* 5.27):

Those who are engaged in prospecting for gold gather rocks along streams, work the lumps which hold the gold dust, and by repeated washing remove the dirt and rocks. Then they place it in a smelter. They acquire great amounts of gold in this way and use it for various types of jewelry—not just women but men as well. On their wrists and arms they wear bracelets, around their necks they wear thick gold rings. They also have delicate golden finger rings and even tunics made of gold.

Diodorus continues with a description of Gaulish women and sexual relations among men (5.32):

Gaulish women are not only equal to the men in size, but they are a match for them in strength as well.

The women of the Gauls are very beautiful, but nevertheless the men strongly prefer to have sex with other males. The usual custom for the men is to sleep on top of animal skins surrounded by bedmates who all roll around together on the ground. The oddest thing about the whole business is that the young men don't care at all about appearances and will gladly give their bodies to anyone. They don't think of this as shameful at all, but rather are highly offended when anyone refuses them.

Strabo's brief comment on gender roles in ancient Gaul is intriguing, though unfortunately he does not elaborate (*Geography* 4.4.3):

Concerning men and women, the tasks which each sex performs is the opposite of that found in our society, but this is common among barbarian peoples.

* * *

In his *Gallic War*, Caesar briefly describes some aspects of marriage and family life among the ancient Gauls, including features of surprising equality and fearsome inequality (6.18–19):

One primary difference between Gauls and Romans is that Gaulish fathers do not allow themselves to be seen in public with their sons until the young men are old enough to serve as warriors. It is considered a disgrace for a father to be seen outside the home with his young son.

When a man marries, he takes the dowry he has received from his wife and matches the amount with money of his own. This money is invested, with careful records kept, so that whichever of the two survives the other receives both amounts plus all interest.

Men also have the power of life and death over their wives and children. When the father who is head of the household dies, if he is of noble birth, all his relatives will come together and examine whether there is any question of a suspicious death. If they discover anything questionable, they will burn and torture his wife to death as if she were a slave.

* * *

The Roman historian Tacitus tells us of the British queen Boudicca, who at the death of her husband in A.D. 60, took effective political control (*Annals* 14.31):

The king of the Iceni, Prasutagus, was long famous for his property. Before he died he had named as his heirs both of his daughters and the Roman emperor. He believed this would ensure safety for his family and kingdom, but he was very wrong. His tribe was treated as a conquered people by the army and his family abused by agents of the government. At the very start, his wife Boudicca was lashed and his daughters raped. Then the leaders of the Iceni had their lands stripped away while the relatives of Prasutagus were treated like slaves. Because of these outrages and fear of even worse treatment to come, the Iceni rose in revolt and persuaded the Trinobantes tribe and others not yet broken by Rome to fight for their freedom.

The revolt against the Romans went well at first, but soon Boudicca and her army faced the full force of the Roman army at a final battle (14.35):

Boudicca mounted her chariot with her daughters beside her and rode throughout the army, rousing them to fight for final victory. "It is not unusual for Britons to follow a woman as leader into war. But I fight not as a queen of glorious lineage to regain my kingdom and power, but as a simple woman of the people who has lost her freedom like a slave, felt the lash of cruel masters, and seen her daughters violated before her very eyes. Roman greed and desire are so powerful that not even their young age and virginity protected them. But the gods have favored us in our vengeance—one legion destroyed in battle while the rest hid behind their camp walls, looking for a way of escape. They wouldn't even come near enough to hear the roar of our troops let alone face our army in battle until now. If they have considered our mighty force of arms and the causes of this war, then they should know that they had better win or die in the attempt. But this is what I as a woman want—that they live to be slaves themselves.

But in the end, as always, Roman might destroyed even the fiercest Celtic spirit. The British army was destroyed and Boudicca took her own life rather than live under Roman control.

* * *

Ammianus Marcellinus is one of the last of the classical writers to discuss Celtic women, but he draws on earlier sources in a passage on Celtic women as warriors. Ammianus is certainly enjoying a bit of exaggeration, but there is no reason to doubt that Gaulish women did occasionally join their men in battle (*History* 15.12.1):

Almost all the Gauls are tall, fair and ruddy in complexion, have terrible flashing eyes, love quarreling, and are amazingly insolent. If one of them in a battle calls out for help to his wife, who with her piercing eyes is stronger than him by far, not even a whole troop of foreigners can stand up to them. This is especially true when, swelling her neck, she starts to pound them with her huge white arms and mixes in fierce kicks with her blows, hitting her enemies with the power of a catapult.

Ammianus also comments on the loud voices and unusual cleanliness of both Gaulish men and women (15.12.2):

Most of them have voices which are both strong and threatening, whether they are happy or angry. And all the Gauls take great pains to always stay clean, especially in the southwestern part of the country. Unlike elsewhere in the world, no man or woman, no matter how poor, is ever seen in dirty or ragged clothes.

THE WESTERN ISLES

The Greek and Roman authors never called the inhabitants of Britain or Ireland *Celts*, but they certainly were aware of the cultural connections between the British and Irish and the Celts of continental Europe. Tacitus speaks of the common language and religion of the Gauls and British, as well as the similarities between the British and Irish. Comparisons of reports on the ancient Gauls with medieval Irish and Welsh tales also show many similarities, though we must always take care in using such evidence. Feasting, common gods, the heroic ethos—all are found throughout the Celtic world, including the islands of Britain and Ireland, from classical times to the Middle Ages. But it is language which shows most clearly the relation between the Celts of the continent and those of the islands. Irish and Welsh, still spoken today along with Scottish Gaelic and Breton, are linguistic relatives of the ancient Celtic languages.

Our knowledge of the ancient Britons and Irish through classical sources is not extensive. We are often restricted to a few casual references on geography or a short description of tribes viewed as either enemies or hopelessly backwards barbarians. Still, what we have can provide some very valuable information about these insular Celts on the edge of the ancient world.

* * *

The earliest classical reference to the British and Irish may in fact be the earliest reference to any of the ancient Celts. In the fourth century A.D., a Roman proconsul named Rufius Avienus wrote a rambling poem known as the *Ora maritima* about a voyage along the Atlantic coast which draws on sources dating perhaps as early as 500 B.C. These sources may include an anonymous *periplus* (coastal description) from the Greek colony at Massalia and the reports of the Carthaginian admiral Himilco. If the documents which Avienus used do go so far back in time, we have a remarkably early Mediterranean view of the British Isles (as both Britain and Ireland together have been known since earliest antiquity). The following brief passage of Avienus describes sailing from the Oestrymnides islands (off the Brittany coast?) to the turf-rich Sacred Isle of the *Hierni* (Irish) and the nearby *Albiones* (British). The Pillars of Hercules demarcate the Strait of Gibraltar at the Atlantic entrance to the Mediterranean Sea, with the ancient city of Tartessus lying on the southwestern coast of the Iberian peninsula (*Ora maritima* 108–19):

> From here it is a voyage of two days
> to the Sacred Isle (for thus the ancients called it),
> rich in turf among the waves.
> The Hierni live there, thickly populating the land,
> and nearby lies the isle of the Albiones.
> The people of Tartessus used to sail even
> to the ends of the Oestrymnides islands.
> The Carthaginians and those dwelling near
> the Pillars of Hercules also sailed those waters.
> Four months is scarcely time for the return voyage,
> as Himilco himself proved by sailing there and back again.

* * *

The Greek navigator Pytheas of Massalia sailed through the Pillars of Hercules in the late fourth century B.C. and explored the Atlantic coast of Gaul, circumnavigated Britain, and perhaps even reached Iceland or Norway. His book *On the Ocean*, now lost, was derided unfairly in antiquity by many scholars as nothing but fiction, though his geographic figures for Britain are certainly too great. Scattered fragments of his descriptions of Britain survive in later ancient writers such as Strabo (*Geography* 1.4.3, 2.4.1):

But Pytheas says the length of the island of Britain is more than 2,300 miles and that Kent is several days sail from Gaul.

After claiming that he traveled the whole of Britain which was accessible, Pytheas reported that the coastline of the island is more than 4,600 miles.

* * *

In the middle of Julius Caesar's long campaign to conquer Gaul, he invaded Britain twice, in 55 and 54 B.C., though he never intended to establish a permanent Roman presence there. His intent was to discourage the Britons from aiding the Gauls in their struggle against Rome. Several passages in his *Gallic War* discuss not only his military struggles against the British, but also their contact with outsiders, customs, dress, and religion. His preparations for the first invasion begin late in the summer of 55 B.C. (4.20):

Only a small part of the summer was remaining for Caesar. In these regions, as in all of northern Gaul, the climate is unlike the south and the winters come early. Even so, Caesar was determined to launch an expedition against Britain. He knew that the Britons had aided the Gauls in almost every uprising against Rome. Although there wasn't time to make a full-fledged war against Britain, Caesar thought it would be advantageous to at least land on the island, learn something of the character of the inhabitants, and reconnoiter the countryside, harbors, and landing places. All these things were almost unknown to the Gauls, since no one except merchants went there without a very good reason, and even the merchants only knew the seacoast and area opposite Gaul. He had summoned to his headquarters merchants from everywhere but could not find out the size of the island, nor which tribes there were and how large each was, nor how the inhabitants fought in battle, nor anything about their internal organization—not even which harbors could handle a large fleet.

Caesar then made preparations for a quick campaign in

Britain by sending one of his lieutenants to scout out the coast and by making compacts of friendship with several British tribes who seemed amiable. He then set sail, but found a hostile reception waiting for him in Britain. This included chariot warfare, which was an archaic form of fighting out of fashion even in Gaul at this time and known to the Romans only from the poet Homer (4.24):

But the Britons, recognizing the strategy of the Romans, sent forward their cavalry and chariots, a type of warfare which they traditionally used in battle. With the rest of their forces following, they attempted to prevent our troops from landing. It was very difficult for the Roman troops to disembark since the ships were too large to approach the shore closely except in deep water. The Romans did not know the terrain at all and their hands were full of heavy weapons, yet they had to leap down from the ships, avoid being knocked over by the waves, and fight the enemy all at the same time. On the other hand, the Britons stood on dry land or just a little way in the water with their hands free. They knew the location well and their horses were trained for this type of battle. Our troops were terrified by all of this and, used to battles on land, did not fight with their accustomed intensity.

After a fierce battle, the Romans landed in Britain and gained the upper hand against the natives. But Caesar suffered numerous setbacks during his short campaign, including encounters with the novelties of chariot warfare, which Caesar describes (4.33):

Their method of fighting from chariots is as follows. First, they rush in against an enemy from all directions hurling their spears and causing general panic and confusion with the noise of the wheels. Then the chariots work their way in between troops of cavalry and the warriors jump off to fight on foot. The charioteers meanwhile move away from the battle slowly and position themselves so that they can easily remove the warriors if necessary. In this way chariot warfare has both the mobility of cavalry and the stability of infantry in battle. By daily practice, the British become so accomplished at this form of warfare that they can gallop their chariot teams down steep slopes without losing control and can turn them at a moment's notice. They can even jump onto the pole between the horses, stand on the yoke, and rush back again into the chariot.

Caesar withdrew his troops from Britain soon thereafter, but returned the next year to conduct a more lengthy and successful campaign reaching the area of modern London. He pauses in his narration of that invasion to describe the British people and the geography of their island (5.12–14):

The interior regions of Britain are occupied by tribes whose own traditions say they are indigenous. The parts of the island near the sea are occupied by tribes who migrated at an earlier time from Belgic Gaul to seek plunder. Nearly all of these maritime tribes call themselves after the names of their original tribes in Gaul. After their invasion they chose to stay behind and establish themselves on the land. The island is thickly populated, with houses very similar to those in Gaul, and cattle are abundant there. They use bronze and gold coins, or ingots of iron of an established weight. Tin is mined in the center of the country, while iron is found in limited quantities in the coastal regions. They import their bronze from abroad. They have every type of tree known in Gaul except for beech and pine. They think it sacrilegious to eat rabbits, chickens, and geese, but they keep all of these as pets. The climate is moderate, with warmer winters than in Gaul.

Britain is shaped like a triangle with one side facing Gaul. One corner of this triangle is the area of Kent facing east, where almost all the ships from Gaul land, and the other corner faces south. This side facing Gaul is about five hundred Roman miles long. . . . Aside from Ireland, several small islands lie near Britain where it is said the midnight sun lasts for thirty days. We could not confirm this through inquiries, but we did measurements with a water clock and found that the summer nights in Britain are shorter than those on the continent. The western side of Britain is said by the natives to be seven hundred miles long. The third side, about eight hundred miles long, has no land near it but in general faces towards Germany. Thus the whole island is about two thousand miles in circumference.

Of all the Britons, the tribes inhabiting the coastal land of Kent are the most civilized, differing little from the Gauls. Most of those in the interior of Britain don't even sow grain, but live on milk and meat, clothing themselves in animal skins. All the Britons dye their skin with woad, which produces a bluish color and makes them appear horrifying in battle. They have long hair and shave every part of their bodies except for the head and upper lip. Groups of ten or twelve men have wives in common, especially brothers with brothers and fathers with sons. When children are born under these arrangements, they are said to belong to the man of the particular house to which the mother was brought when she first joined the group.

* * *

A few decades later, but before the Roman conquest, Strabo describes a personal encounter with Britons (*Geography* 4.5.2):

The Britons are taller and slimmer than the Celts of Gaul and not so blond. The following is an example of their size—in Rome, I myself saw some British men who were at least half a foot taller than everyone else, even though they were bowlegged and slouched.

* * *

During his description of the Roman attack on the Welsh island of Anglesey in A.D. 60, the Roman historian Tacitus gives us one of the few descriptions of Druids outside of Gaul (*Annals* 14.30):

On the opposite shore was the densely packed army of the enemy. Around their ranks were women dressed like the Furies, running around with wild hair waving sticks. Everywhere the Druids were raising prayers to the sky and calling down curses, the sight of which terrified our men, who had never seen such a thing before. They stood there exposed to the enemy's weapons as if their legs and arms were paralyzed. But thanks to mutual encouragement and to the urging of their commander not to be scared of a bunch of crazy women, they soon pressed forward, crushing and burning all resistance. A garrison was left there which destroyed their groves dedicated to savage superstition. For the Druids considered it their sacred duty to cover their altars with human blood and consult the gods by studying human entrails.

Tacitus, in his biography of his father-in-law the Roman general Agricola, also records some of our most detailed information on the geography, tribes, and customs of the Britons during the first century A.D. Agricola was military governor of Britain from A.D. 77–84, during which time he advanced Roman power and control, at least temporarily, from southern Britain into the central and northern parts of the island as far as the Orkney Islands and Caledonia in northern Scotland.

The first passage deals with Roman geographical knowledge of Britain. Some of the facts are plainly wrong, as when he continues an old tradition placing Britain opposite Spain, but some claims, such as the extent of tides inland in Scotland, must be based on Agricola's firsthand reports. The Thule mentioned by Tacitus is probably the Shetland Islands (*Agricola* 10):

Even though the geography of Britain and its population have been described by many earlier writers, I shall discuss them here again, not to compare my meager skills to theirs, but because they were forced by a lack of knowledge to adorn their writings with unsupported speculations. I on the other hand will offer facts based on recent discoveries. Britain is the largest island known to the Romans, facing Germany in the east, Spain on the west, and on the south it lies within sight of Gaul. The northern coast of the island lies opposite no land, but is beaten by a huge and open sea. The shape of Britain has been compared to an oblong rhombus or a double-headed axe by Livy and Fabius Rusticus, the best of ancient and modern writers, respectively. The shape of Britain south of Caledonia is indeed like this, and so writers have assumed the whole island is of the same shape. But when you continue north you will find a huge and rugged mass of land shaped like a wedge which eventually tapers off into the sea. This shore was just recently circumnavigated by a Roman fleet, proving once and for all that Britain is indeed an island. At the same time the Roman ships discovered and subjugated a group of previously unknown islands called the Orkneys. Thule was also sighted, but no attempt was made at landing as they had no orders and winter was fast approaching. But some writers say that the ocean in this region is thick and heavy for rowers, not even rising up in high winds like other seas. I suppose this is because there are no mountains or land there, which are the cause of storms, and thus the huge mass of the sea is very slow to rise. The nature of the Ocean and tides is outside my subject matter for this book, but I will add one interesting fact: nowhere else does the sea have such great power. Not only does the great tidal mass pound the shores, but it penetrates far inland, pushing the ebb and flow of the tides among the highlands and mountains as if in its own realm.

Tacitus continues with a discussion of British ethnography, noting especially the cultural, religious, and linguistic similarities between the Britons and inhabitants of Gaul (11):

Who were the first inhabitants of Britain? Were they an indigenous people or invaders from beyond the sea? As with so many barbarians, it is difficult to say for certain. The physical characteristics of the Britons vary and this variety hints at their origins. The red hair and the large limbs of the Caledonians suggest a Germanic origin, while the dark faces and curly hair of the Silures and the fact that Spain lies nearby argues that at some time in the past this area was settled by immigrants crossing over from Spain. Those Britons nearest the Gauls resemble them either because of common origin or similar climate in these regions so close together. It seems very likely that the Gauls at some point settled in Britain. The religious beliefs of the two lands are the same and there is hardly any difference in their languages. There is also the same quality of recklessness in seeking out danger and the same cowardliness when it actually appears. But the Britons are braver than the Gauls, because they have not been pacified for as long. We know that the Gauls too once were fearless in war, but the sluggishness that comes with peace has made them soft. Their bravery vanished along with their freedom. The Britons who were conquered first are the same way, the rest remain as the Gauls once were.

Tacitus next addresses British chariot warfare, along with political disorder, climate, agriculture, and natural resources (12):

The strength of the Britons is in their infantry. Some tribes also use chariots in war, with a nobleman driving and his supporters fighting alongside him. In the past the Britons obeyed kings, but now they are split into factions and groups led by petty chiefs. Of course, nothing has been more useful to us in their conquest than their lack of cooperation with each other. It is a rare thing for two or three tribes to unite in repelling a common danger—each fights us alone and so we defeat them all. The climate of Britain is dreadful with frequent rain and clouds, but at least the winters are not bitterly cold. The days are longer than in our southern regions and the nights are so short in the northern parts of the island that you would have a hard time distinguishing the end of one day and the beginning of the next. If there are no clouds covering the sky, the glow of the sun can be seen all night long, not rising or setting but passing along the southern horizon. The reason for this must be that the flat extremities of the earth cast low shadows and do not raise up the darkness, so that night fails to reach the sky and the stars. The soil of Britain produces good crops, except for olives, grapes, and other fruits which grow only in warmer climates. The plants spring forth quickly but are slow to ripen due to the wet climate. Britain also has gold, silver, and other metals which have made it worth conquering. The surrounding sea produces pearls as well of a grayish-blue color. The natives, according to some, are not skilled in collecting these even though they are cast up on shore by the sea, unlike the pearls of the Indian Ocean which must be gathered alive and breathing from the rocks. Personally, I find it easier to believe that the quality of the pearls is lacking, not the natives' greed.

Much of the remainder of the *Agricola* is devoted to the Roman conquest of northern England, southern Scotland, and eastern Caledonia, culminating in the battle of Mount Graupius in A.D. 84. This last great battle between Roman and Celtic armies is seen, of course, from the Roman point of view, but it is surprisingly sympathetic to the British and, as shown in the speech of the British leader Calgacus, remarkably critical of Roman power. Even though there is little reason to think that Tacitus reproduces the genuine words of Calgacus, the passage gives us an important view of the Celts through Roman eyes (29–33):

Agricola at last reached Mount Graupius, which he found occupied by the enemy. The British were not broken by their previous defeat, but were ready for either revenge or enslavement. They had finally learned that a common danger must be faced by common and coordinated resistance, and so had sent around delegates and drawn up agreements to bring together the military forces of all the tribes. And now over thirty thousand armed men could be seen, with all the young men still streaming in to join the army as well as older veterans, still fearsome, wearing their own well-earned decorations of successful battles. Among the British leaders Calgacus stood out by both his high birth and proven courage. It is said that before the assembled throng eager for battle he spoke as follows:

"When I consider our reasons for fighting and our present position here, I feel in my very soul that our common action will today be the beginning of liberty for all of Britain. For all of you have come here as free men, not slaves. There is no land of refuge beyond and even the sea is ruled by the Roman fleet. Thus battle it is—an event always welcome to the brave and even now the safest course of action to even the fearful. Earlier battles against the Romans were fought with various fortune, but no matter the outcome the Britons always knew that we were here in reserve. We, the most noble and bravest men of Britain, were yet hidden away in these remote hills, warriors not gazing out at any lands held in Roman slavery with our eyes free from the defiling sight of tyranny. To this day the very remoteness and obscurity of our land have defended us, the most distant inhabitants of the earth and the last of free men. But no more. Now the most remote part of Britain lies open, with men assuming that any unknown place must hold vast riches. Behind us there is nothing but rocks and waves, in front of us are the Romans even more deadly. You would throw yourselves on the tender mercies of the Romans in vain. They are despoilers of the earth, turning their sight even on the sea when they have devastated the land. A rich enemy excites their greed, a poor enemy their lust for power and control. East and West have not satisfied them yet, for they alone of all people desire to rule both the wealthy and the poor. They rob their subjects, they slaughter the innocent, they seize whatever they want, all under the false name of 'good government,' when in truth they have made the world a desert and called it peace.

It is the very nature of a person to love family and children above all else. These are now being taken from the Britons and carried away into other lands. Our wives and sisters, even if they escape the lustful soldiers, are defiled by those Romans who later come as our supposed friends and guests. Our goods and what money we have are consumed by Roman taxes, every year our crops go to fill their granaries, our bodies themselves are worn down in manual labor with lashes and insults to fortify forests and swamps. Some nations are born to be slaves, but even they are sold only once and are at least fed by their masters. But Britain sells itself into slavery every day and must feed its own Roman masters as well. And just as in a household the most recently acquired slave is abused by his fellow slaves, we, the newest and most reviled servants in a world long ago enslaved, are marked out for destruction. Britain has no fertile fields, no rich mines, no bustling ports in which we might be spared to labor. Indeed, our very courage and bravery are held against us by our masters. Our very remoteness and isolation, which for so long have protected us, make us that much more suspect to them. Therefore, with all hope of Roman mercy and kindness removed, I say take up your arms! Fight for your honor or your life, whichever you hold most dear. With even a woman as leader the British once managed to destroy a Roman colony and wipe out a legionary camp. They would have been able to throw off the yoke of Roman oppression entirely if only they hadn't grown careless. We on the other hand are free men, never knowing Roman rule and not fighting merely for revenge but freedom itself. So let us crush them even in the first moments of battle, for we are the finest warriors in all of Caledonia!

Come now, do you really think that Roman courage in war matches their wantonness in time of peace? They are so often victorious because of dissention among their enemies on which they build the supposedly great reputation of their military. The Roman army is a conglomeration of various nations which holds together as long as things go their way, but it will fall to pieces when events turn against them. Do you seriously think that the Gauls and Germans, as well as some Britons I'm ashamed to say, are shedding their life's blood for the Romans out of loyalty and affection? They were enemies of Rome for much longer than they have been her allies. Fear and terror are poor bonds of friendship, and when you can break these bonds, then fear ends and hatred will begin. We have every incitement for victory on our side, while the Romans have no wives here to encourage them, no parents to chasten them if they flee from battle. Most of them can't even remember their homeland and if they can, it is a place other than Rome. They are few in number and fearful because of the unfamiliar climate, sea, and forests. Everything they see is strange and unknown to them. The gods have trapped them and handed the Romans over to us. Don't be afraid of their pretty-boy appearance and nice, shiny armor. Silver and gold never killed anyone. And in the very ranks of the enemy we will find helping hands. The Britons will recognize our cause as their own and the Gauls will remember their former freedom. Other Germans besides the Usipi who recently deserted will also turn on their Roman masters. And there isn't any great defense lying beyond this mountain—the legionary camps are empty, the veteran colonies are made up only of old men, and the weak cities to the south contain only discontented subjects and unjust rulers. Here you have your own leader, here you have an army—there you will find only crushing taxes, labor in the mines, and the other burdens of slavery. You must choose whether you will serve them forever or seize victory here and now. And as you go into battle, remember all those who went before you and all those who will follow."

This speech was received in a typically barbarian fashion, with shouting and singing and a general chaotic clamor. The battle-line immediately began to take shape, with a flash of weapons and even some of the most audacious warriors charging the Romans on their own.

Agricola also gave a speech encouraging his own troops, then the fighting began. The battle itself, with its gaudy chariot drivers, fearless Britons, and methodically ruthless Romans, is a fitting finale to the long struggle of the Celts against the legions of Rome (35–38):

The British army was positioned on the high ground in a way designed to impress and terrify our forces. Their front line was on the level plain, but the rear lines rose in close formation up the slopes of the mountain. Between the two camps the British charioteers rushed about in a noisy display.

The battle began with an exchange of spears. The Britons showed great skill avoiding and deflecting our spears with their huge swords and small shields, while they showered us with a volley of spears in return. Then Agricola ordered four Batavian cohorts and two of the Tungri to advance and attack the British at close quarters with their swords. These cohorts were experienced at such fighting and the British were not, since their native swords had no points and were useless in cramped combat which involved thrusting rather than swinging their swords. So the Batavians came at them relentlessly, struck them with their shield bosses, and stabbed at their faces. This began to drive those who had been stationed on the level plain up onto the slopes of the hill. The other Roman cohorts were inspired when they saw this and began to attack the enemy nearest them, with many injured Britons, and even some not wounded, left behind by their comrades due to our rapid advance.

At this time, since the British chariots had fled, our cavalry plunged headlong into the middle of the infantry battle. At first they terrified the enemy, but because of the uneven ground and densely packed ranks of foot soldiers, our cavalry rapidly became stuck in the middle of a fight not suited for horses. Our infantry also had only a precarious foothold and were being jostled constantly by the horses. To make matters worse, runaway chariot teams or riderless horses were constantly running into our troops head-on or smashing into them from the side.

Meanwhile, the British troops on the top of the hill, who had so far not taken part in the action, gazed down contemptuously at our smaller forces. They then started to slowly move down the hill and began to encircle our army's rear. Agricola had been afraid that this might happen and immediately sent four squadrons of reserve cavalry against their flanking movement. Their attack had begun with great spirit, but it soon turned into a panicked retreat. The same plan of the British was soon used against them as our squadrons, obedient to orders, moved from the front of the battle and attacked the British rear. Then you would have seen a most grim and awesome spectacle. Our cavalry chased the retreating British, struck down many and captured others, then killed these prisoners as they overtook more of the enemy. Some cowardly groups of well-armed British warriors ran away in the face of inferior numbers, while others bravely sought death by throwing themselves unarmed into the middle of the Romans. Weapons, bodies, and severed limbs lay everywhere on the bloody earth. Some of the defeated British managed to find their courage again when they reached the woods. Knowing the location well, they gathered together and ambushed the first of our soldiers to pursue them into the trees. This might have led to a disaster for our overconfident troops if it weren't for Agricola's clear thinking. He ordered strong cohorts of light infantry to surround the British as if they were hunting wild beasts. Cavalry was used in the more open areas, but where the woods were thick he ordered dismounted troops to scour the forest. When the British saw our troops in organized pursuit, they turned and ran, not in any order as before but with no one looking out for his comrades. They avoided gathering in groups and sought out distant and trackless places. The coming of darkness ended the scattered fighting, along with the fact that the Romans had finally had enough of killing. Ten thousand British soldiers died compared with only three hundred and sixty Roman troops. Among these was Aulus Atticus, a young prefect of a cohort, who was carried to his death deep in the ranks of the enemy by youthful bravery and an overly spirited horse.

For the victors it was a night of rejoicing and dividing the spoils of war. The British men and women wandered through the night weeping, carrying away their wounded, and calling out to other survivors. They deserted their homes and even set fire to them. In their confusion they hid in the shadows, then immediately sought shelter elsewhere. They tried to make plans for the future, but then drifted away. Some were broken-hearted at the sight of their loved ones, but more often they were enraged at their prospects in defeat. We know for certain that some men even killed their own wives and children in a kind of pity.

The light of the next day showed fully the results of victory. Everywhere was a vast silence. The hills were deserted, houses smoldered in the distance, and the British had disappeared.

* * *

We have already seen how the fourth-century A.D. author Avienus may have drawn on sources dating back to 500 B.C. in his description of Britain and Ireland. But we hear nothing more of Ireland in the classical sources for over four hundred years, when in the first century B.C. Diodorus Siculus makes a passing reference to the cannibals of *Iris* (probably Ireland) in his history of the world. They are here called *Prettanoi*, an early name for the inhabitants of the British Isles. Charges of cannibalism among distant tribes are found as early as Homer and Herodotus and are a commonplace slur in classical descriptions of barbarians at the edges of the civilized world (5.32.3):

The most savage people are those living in the north as well as those who border Scythia. Some report that they eat human flesh, as do the Prettanoi who dwell in Iris.

* * *

In Julius Caesar's description of his invasion of Britain in 54 B.C., he gives a brief geographical description of Ireland, which he calls *Hibernia*. This first certain reference to Ireland is simple, but generally accurate. Caesar also is the first to mention *Mona* (the Isle of Man or possibly Anglesey) lying between Britain and Ireland (*Gallic War* 5.13):

The second side of Britain faces Spain and the setting sun, in which direction also is Ireland, which is estimated to be roughly half the size of Britain. It is separated from Britain by the same distance as Britain is separated from Gaul. In the sea midway between Britain and Ireland is an island called Mona.

* * *

Strabo mistakenly places Ireland (which he calls *Ierne*) far above Britain and sees it as the northernmost habitable land in the world. To Strabo, a cold and wretched climate must produce totally uncivilized people, so the Irish are presented once again as cannibals with absolutely no morals, like the Scythians in northern Asia. But at least he is honest enough to admit he has no hard evidence for this characterization (*Geography* 2.5.8, 4.5.4):

Modern writers have nothing to say about any lands beyond Ireland, which lies to the north of Britain. The people who live there are completely wild and have a miserable existence on account of the cold weather. I believe that there is no habitable land to the north of Ireland.

There are other small islands around Britain. The largest of these is Ireland, which lies to the north of Britain and is longer than it is wide. Concerning this island I have nothing certain to say, only that the inhabitants are even more uncivilized than those of Britain. The Irish are both cannibals and gluttons. They quite openly eat their dead fathers and have sex with any woman they can find, even their mothers and sisters. I don't really have any reliable reports of this kind of behavior, but we know that the Scythians are cannibals and even the Celts, Iberians, and many others will eat each other out of necessity if their cities are under siege.

* * *

Pomponius Mela briefly mentions Ireland in his description of the world written about A.D. 44. The climate of the island has certainly improved since Strabo, but the inhabitants were still thought of as savages (*De chorographia* 3.53):

The climate of Ireland is favorable for growing grain. The grass there is so thick and sweet that cattle let out into the fields can eat their fill in a only a short time and would burst if they were not restrained. The Irish are uncivilized, utterly without regard for duty or justice, and in general more ignorant of decent values than any people on earth.

* * *

The *Agricola* of Tacitus contains a brief but very important passage on ancient Ireland set midway through the Roman conquest of northern England and southern Scotland in A.D. 82. In it he relates how his father-in-law Agricola used to speculate on how easy and desirable the Roman conquest of Ireland would be. Agricola even made tentative preparations for an invasion, fortifying the coast and keeping in his entourage a refugee Irish king, the only individual Irish person known from antiquity. The passage provides important evidence, confirmed by archaeology, of a Roman trade network reaching into Ireland (24):

In the fourth year of the British campaign, Agricola crossed in the lead ship into the territory of previously unknown tribes and won frequent battles against them. He also set up garrisons in that part of Britain facing Ireland, but this was more from hope of an upcoming invasion than fear of Irish raids. It would be very useful if Ireland, located midway between Britain and Spain and also accessible to the Gallic Sea, could join together the strongest parts of the Empire. Ireland is rather narrow compared to Britain, but it is still larger than any island in the Mediterranean Sea. In respect to climate, fertility of the soil, and the customs of the inhabitants, it is very similar to Britain. The approaches and ports are well known thanks to merchants. Agricola used to keep with him on the campaign an Irish king who had fled his homeland due to some internal struggle with the hope that he might find him useful some day. I often heard Agricola say that he could conquer Ireland with just one legion and a moderate number of auxiliary troops. And indeed it would be desirable as a lesson to Britain if it were surrounded by Roman forces on all sides and liberty were banished from its sight.

* * *

The early second-century A.D. poet and social critic Juvenal contrasts the degenerate moral state of those dwelling in Rome with the victorious achievements of the Roman army. Although some have been tempted to see this passage as a reference to a supposed Roman invasion of Ireland, it is much more reasonable to see it as a typical example of hyperbole in Roman satirical poetry (*Satire* 2.159–161):

> Our armies have even advanced
> beyond the shores of Ireland
> and the recently captured Orkneys
> and the fierce Britons with their short nights.

* * *

Claudius Ptolemy, who wrote his *Geography* in the middle of the second century A.D., provides us with more information on Ireland than any other classical author. Unfortunately, most of what he wrote consists of bare lists of prominent physical features such as river mouths, towns, and tribal names. While these are important, he tells us nothing of Irish culture, language, or religion. One passage, however, reinforces Tacitus' statement on Roman merchant visits to Ireland and suggests the sources of Ptolemy's information were earlier geographers who received their information from traders (1.11):

Marinus does not believe the reports of merchants, at least not the account that it takes twenty days to cross Ireland from east to west, because Philemon says he heard this from tradesmen.

Ptolemy's map of Ireland is quite accurate given his limited knowledge. A few of the many features Ptolemy lists are as follows (2.1):

> The mouth of the *Senu* river (the Shannon River)
> The mouth of the *Birgu* river (Waterford harbor?)
> The town of *Eblana* (near modern Dublin)
> The mouth of the *Buwinda* river (the river Boyne)
> The inland town of *Dunon* (Irish for "fortress")

* * *

The Roman writer Solinus produced a gossipy and altogether fanciful collection of stories from various parts of the world about A.D. 200, including a small section on supposed remarkable facts about Ireland. He repeats the story of voracious cattle from Pomponius Mela, continues the tradition of Irish savagery, and, over two hundred years before St. Patrick reportedly drove them out, reveals that there are no snakes in Ireland (*Collectanea rerum memorabilium* 22.2–5):

Many important islands surround Britain, of which Ireland is the nearest in size. The rituals of the inhabitants are inhuman, but the land itself is very fertile, so that cattle not brought in from the fields in time would excessively gorge themselves. There are no snakes there and very few birds. The people of the island are inhospitable and warlike, draining the blood of their foes and smearing it on their own faces. They have absolutely no sense of right and wrong. There have never been any bees there. Moreover, if anyone sprinkles Irish soil or pebbles around beehives elsewhere, the bees will abandon their honeycombs.

* * *

After Solinus, we hear nothing of Ireland in the classical writers for almost a century. When reports begin again in the fourth century, writers speak of raids by the barbarous *Scotti* (a new name for the Irish) on Roman Britain, along with harassment by Picts, Attacotti, and Saxons. Ammianus Marcellinus speaks of a series of raids in the 360's (*History* 20.1.1, 26.4.5, 27.8.5):

In the tenth consulship of the emperor Constantius and the third consulship of Julian, an invasion of savage Scotti and Pictish tribes ravaged Britain. The peace which had been arranged was broken and the areas along the frontier were devastated. The British, worn down by the frequent disasters of the past, were filled with terror.

At this time, as if war trumpets were sounding throughout the whole of the Empire, savage tribes poured across the borders nearest to each. Gaul and Raetia were attacked at the same time by the Alamanni and Britain faced constant harassment from the Picts, Saxons, Scotti, and Attacotti.

It is enough to say that at that time the Picts, divided into the Dicalydones and Verturiones, along with the warlike nation of the Attacotti and the Scotti, were ranging far and wide in their raids.

* * *

The early Church father and biblical translator St. Jerome speaks briefly of the Irish in a colorful and unflattering description of *c.* A.D. 390. As a young man, Jerome spent time in Gaul where he claims to have encountered Scotti cannibals. How seriously we should take this charge is open to debate, especially since Jerome seems predisposed to a traditionally barbaric view of the Irish (*Adversus Jovinianum* 2.7):

But why should I speak of other nations when I myself as a young man in Gaul saw Scotti, a people of the British Isles, eating human flesh? Whenever the Scotti come across pig herders or their wives in the woods, they will frequently cut off their buttocks and nipples, thinking that these alone are great delicacies. The Scotti also do not have individual wives, but share women among each other as if they had read Plato's *Republic* or were following the example of Cato. Truly, they are nothing but beasts.

* * *

One of the last classical writers to mention Ireland is the Roman senator Symmachus, who in a letter of *c.* A.D. 393 notes that huge Scotti dogs (Irish wolfhounds?) had been shipped to Rome for the public games (*Epistle* 2.77):

Seven Scotti dogs were shown in the parade before the games, creatures which so amazed the Romans that they thought the beasts must have been imported in iron cages.

* * *

Tradition says that St. Patrick arrived in Ireland in A.D. 432 to begin his missionary activities. Whether or not that date is correct, Patrick serves as a fitting transition between the classical world and the early medieval age in Ireland. Born into a family of moderate wealth in late Roman Britain, Patrick was kidnapped by slave traders and taken to Ireland, where he served his masters as a shepherd for several years before escaping. He later returned to Ireland as a bishop and began the conversion of the Irish to Christianity. The troubles he faced were many, including the lack of a proper education, physical threats to his life, even opposition and charges of corruption from jealous Church officials outside Ireland. His autobiographical *Confession* (selections of which are reproduced below), lacking the later fantastic legends which grew up around his life, reveals the struggles, insecurities, compassion, and amazing drive of a remarkable man (1–2, 6–10, 16–18, 23, 41–42, 52, 61):

I, Patrick, a sinner, am the most unpolished and least important of all the faithful Christians—indeed I am considered contemptible by many of them. My father was Calpornius, a deacon, and my grandfather Potitus, a presbyter, from the village of Bannavem Taberniae. He had a small villa near there, which is where I was captured. I was barely sixteen at the time and ignorant of the true God. I was taken to Ireland along with thousands of others. All of us deserved our fate as we had turned away from God and not kept his commandments. We had ignored the priests, who admonished us concerning our salvation. And the Lord brought upon us the anger of his wrath and scattered us among many nations to the ends of the earth, even to this land where my many failings may be seen by foreigners. It was here that God opened my mind so that I might finally understand my sins and that my heart might be turned to the Lord God. For He took pity on my youth and ignorance, caring for me before I even knew Him. He watched over me before I could distinguish between good and evil, protecting and consoling me as a father does his son.

Though I am imperfect in many ways, I would like my brothers and family to know what kind of person I am, so that they might understand the will of my soul. So for this reason I have long considered writing this defense of myself, but have hesitated until now because I was afraid my ignorance of proper language might offend the learned. For I am not like the better class of people who have studied legal and sacred writings in equal measure and have never had to change the language they learned as children, always improving their skills as they grew. I, on the other hand, have long spoken and shaped my style of speech to fit a foreign tongue, as anyone can easily see from my writing. As the wise man says, "a man's wisdom and understanding and knowledge of the truth will be discovered through his words." But what good does it do to offer excuses even if they are true? It would be presumptuous if as an old man I tried to gain that eloquence which I might have had in my youth if my sins had not prevented me. Who will bother reading my words now even when I say what I have said before? I was captured as a beardless youth, before I knew what manner of style to follow or avoid, so that now I am ashamed and fear exposing my lack of learning. I don't even know how to explain myself concisely in a few words, for even if my spirit is eager, my mind and senses are not up to the task.

After I had been taken to Ireland, I daily tended the flocks and frequently I prayed. My love for God and fear of him grew more and more, as my faith increased and my spirit was stirred within me. In a single day I would say a hundred prayers and at night as well, as I was alone in the forests and on a mountain. Before sunrise I prayed, through snow, frost, and rain. There was no fearfulness in me, as there is now, because my spirit was fervent. And one night I heard a voice say to me, "Your fasting has served you well, for soon you will return to your homeland." And again after a little while I heard a voice saying to me, "Behold, your ship is ready." It was not nearby but two hundred miles away, in a place where I had never been nor did I know anyone there. Soon I fled the man who I had served for six years and trusted myself to God, who directed my path well. I was afraid of nothing until I came to that ship. On the day that I arrived at the harbor the ship was about to leave, so I asked if I might sail with them. But the captain was not pleased and said there was absolutely no way that I was coming along. After I heard this I left them and went to the little hut where I was staying. I began to pray, but even before I had finished my prayer one of the sailors shouted to me to go quickly to them because they were calling for me. So immediately I got up and returned to the ship. They then said to me, "Come on, we'll take you along in good faith. Bind yourself to us in friendship however you wish." But I refused to suck their nipples (a dreadful pagan ritual!) because I feared God. Yet I did hope that some of these pagans might become Christians, so I stayed with them for that reason. And then we set sail.

And after my absence of several years I returned to Britain and was with my family. They received me as a son and begged me, after so many trials and tribulations, never to go away from them. But while I was there, I saw a vision in the night of a man coming as if from Ireland carrying many letters. He handed me one and I read the beginning of the letter entitled "The Voice of the Irish." While I was reading the letter I thought I heard the cries of those Irish who live near the woods of Foclut beside the western sea. They all called out to me as if in one voice, "Holy youth, we beg of you, come and walk among us again." I was struck deeply in my heart and could read no more, so I awoke. Thanks be to God that after so many years the Lord granted them their desire.

It is remarkable that the Irish have indeed become a people of the Lord and are children of God. These people who up 'til now had no knowledge of God, but worshipped idols and followed disgusting religious practices. Now the sons of the Scotti and the daughters of their kings are becoming monks and virgins for Christ. I remember one very special Irish woman of noble birth, full grown and beautiful, whom I myself baptized. A few days later she came to us and told me in confidence that she had received a command from God that she was to become a virgin for Christ and thus draw close to God. Thanks be to God that six days later, with the best of intentions and with great excitement, she indeed accepted that vocation. That is the way it is here with those who would be virgins of God. They do not do so with the blessings of their fathers—far from it. They follow this path in spite of persecution and false accusations from their parents, with their number increasing nevertheless. This does not even include the enslaved British women who were born here, nor the widows and others who live in chastity. Those women who are slaves suffer the most, enduring continual threats and terrors. But God has given grace to many of my handmaidens, for even though they are forbidden, they follow the example set by others.

I admit that sometimes I used to give presents as bribes to the local Irish kings besides the gifts I would give to their sons who accompanied me on my journeys. Even so, there was one occasion when they seized me along with my companions. They wanted to kill me that day, but my time had not yet come. They stole everything we had and bound me in iron chains. But fourteen days later I was freed and all was restored to us, thanks to the intervention of the Lord and to several powerful friends I had made.

I ask those who are believers and fear God, whoever will have taken the time to read these words which Patrick the ignorant sinner wrote in Ireland, that they not credit me with any good work or the act of leading anyone to the Lord. Instead, I hope you will believe truly and firmly that it was a gift of God.

THE ANCIENT CELTS SPEAK

The Greek and Roman authors provide us with the best picture we have of ancient Celtic life, but there is one other type of written evidence available. As we have seen, the Druids forbade the writing of sacred texts, but this does not mean the Celts of classical times were illiterate. We possess scattered bits and pieces of inscriptions written by the Celts themselves in their own languages. These written remains are limited and are very often obscure in meaning, but we can understand enough of most inscriptions to give us some important insights into ancient Celtic life.

The Celtic languages of the classical world were all closely related to each other and, more distantly, to Greek and Latin as part of the great Indo-European family of languages. Lepontic, Celtiberian, Galatian, and Gaulish were all ancient Celtic languages spoken and written in various parts of western Europe and Asia Minor. Other Celtic languages surely existed and thrived at the same time, but we have no written remains of these tongues.

The passages below should be taken only as rough and imperfect translations. As more Celtic inscriptions are uncovered by archaeologists, our knowledge of the languages should increase accordingly.

* * *

The earliest writings we have in any Celtic language are the Lepontic inscriptions from the lake region of northern Italy. Stretching over a period of several centuries, some date perhaps as early as the seventh century B.C. There are over 120 of these inscriptions, most of which are very short and simple funeral dedications on stone or vases. The Lepontic language itself is an early form of Gaulish written in a variety of the north Etruscan alphabet.

Although the translation of Lepontic inscriptions is often uncertain, one dedication engraved on a vase from Ornavasso is fairly clear:

For Latumaros and Sapsuta, Naxian wine

Even at this early date, the common Celtic love of wine is well attested—in this case, the celebrated vintage of Naxos imported from the east coast of Sicily.

Carved on a stone slab, an inscription from Vergiate discovered in 1913 is more problematic:

Deu built this tomb and raised this monument to Belgos

The dedicator, *Deu*, constructed the tomb and erected a memorial stone (*pala*) to *Belgos*, a common Celtic name.

* * *

A second-century B.C. stone from Todi in Umbria shows a similar tradition of memorial stones among the later Gaulish inhabitants of northern Italy (Cisalpine Gaul). This badly damaged double-sided inscription, now in the Vatican Museum, alternates both Latin and Gaulish versions of the text on both sides with only minor variations:

Coisis, son of Drutos, established this memorial of Ategnatos, son of Drutos

Coisis does his fraternal duty for his brother Ategnatos by preparing a memorial. The verb used, *karnitu* ("raise, set up") is related to Welsh *carn*, which has found its way into English as *cairn* ("a heap of stones").

A second- or first-century B.C. stone slab from Vercelli in northern Italy preserves a bilingual Latin-Gaulish dedication of land for religious purposes:

Akisios Argantokomaterekos donated the field to both gods and men

Akisios had apparently done well for himself as he bore the name *Argantokomaterekos*, a mouthful meaning "banker" or "money-lender" (the first element is *arganto-* "silver"). The final word in the original, *tevoxtonion*, probably to be read as *devo-gdonion*, is a wonderful example of a very ancient type of compound, in this case combining elements divine, *devo-* ("gods"), and human, *gdonios* ("those of the earth" or "men")—a relative of Greek *chthonios* ("under the earth"), hence our English word *chthonic*.

* * *

The Galatian invaders of Asia Minor did not leave behind any writing in their native Celtic tongue, but they did soon learn to write in Greek, the lingua franca of the day. The Galatians were fearsome warriors and were famous as mercenary soldiers throughout the eastern Mediterranean. One such band of Galatian fighters in Egypt during the early second century B.C. left a charming bit of graffiti in Greek on a temple of the Egyptian god Horus at Thebes as a testimony to their travels:

The Galatians Thoas, Kallistratos, Akannon, and Apollonios: We came here and caught a fox.

* * *

The Celts of Spain also wrote in their native language known as Celtiberian, or more generally, Hispano-Celtic. One of the longest records in the language is a late second- or early first-century B.C. inscription on a bronze tablet from Botorrita near modern Zaragoza and records regulations for land usage. But a stone carved in Latin script from the mountainous area of Peñalba de Villastar, now in the Archaeological Museum at

Barcelona, with a dedication to the Celtic god Lugus, is per-haps more interesting:

To Eniorosis and Tiato of Tiginos we dedicate *trecaias* and to Lugus we dedicate *arainom*.

To Eniorosis and to Equaesos, *ogris* erects coverings of *olga* and to Lugus he erects coverings of the *tiasos*.

Admittedly, this is a very incomplete and unsatisfactory trans-lation. The god *Lugus* is the one certain feature of the inscrip-tion. He was seen earlier in Caesar as the probable Gaulish equivalent of the Roman Mercury. Lugus is found in many places throughout the ancient Celtic world and survives in Irish folk tradition in the midsummer festival of Lughnasadh—this inscription may suggest a similar festival among the Celts of Iberia.

* * *

Compared to the evidence of ancient Celtic writing from Spain and elsewhere, the inscriptions we have from Gaul are relatively numerous. Unfortunately, they are often just as obscure in their meaning. One intriguing Gaulish inscription from *c.* A.D. 50 is engraved in Roman cursive letters on a lead tablet deposited in a spring at the spa of Chamalières near Clermont-Ferrand in south-central France. It was found in 1971, along with many wooden sculptures of body parts. Lead tablets buried or cast into water were a favorite medium in the ancient world for sending messages, be they invocations or curses, to the deities of the underworld (Gaulish *anderon*). The Chamalières tablet seems to be a prayer offered by a group of men:

I invoke the god Maponos *arueriitis*. Through the magic of the un-derworld gods.

C. Lucios Floros, Nigrinos the speaker, Aemilios Paterinos, Claudios Legitumos, Caelios Pelignos, Claudios Pelignos, Marcios Victorinos, and Asiaticos son of Adsedillos . . .

The oath they will swear—the small shall become great, the crooked become straight, and, though blind, I will see. With this tablet of incantation this will be . . .

luge dessummiiis luge dessumiis luge dessumiiis luxe.

This invocation is made first to the god *Maponos*, seen in later Welsh literature as the divine youth *Mabon*. The threefold parallelism of opposite qualities (*small . . . great, crooked . . . straight, blind . . . see*) and the repetition (untranslated) at the end of the tablet strongly evokes the magical and ritual quality of the prayer.

Another Gaulish inscription found on a lead tablet comes from a woman's grave at Larzac near Millau in southern France. It survives in two pieces with writing on both sides, and dates to approximately A.D. 90. This tablet, like that from Chamalières, contains an invocation with a list of names—but the names from Larzac are of women, not men, and the text suggests a much more fearsome quality, a darker type of magic practiced by these women. Once again, the interpretation of many phrases is quite uncertain, but the general sense of the inscription (just a small part of the first section is given below) shows us that these "women of magic" (Gaulish *bnas brictom*) were not to be taken lightly:

> Behold:
> —a magical incantation of women
> —their ritual underworld names
> —the prophesy of the seeress who weaves this spell
> The goddess Adsagsona renders Severa and Tertionicna
>   enchanted and bound.

This is followed by a list of names of those invoking this magical incantation, most of whom are listed in relationship to another woman as mother or daughter—which may signify a ritual rather than biological bond.

Not all Gaulish texts concern solemn ritual or magical invocations. Some very entertaining and sometimes bawdy inscriptions come from eastern France, many from Autun, engraved on spindle-whorls. These small ceramic weights carried short love messages in Latin, Gaulish, or a mixture of the two languages and are usually addressed to young women. Some of the Latin phrases are simple and charming:

> *Salve tu puella*
> Be well, girl.

> *Ave vale bella tu*
> Hello, goodbye, you're beautiful!

Others are a little more direct:

> *Accede urbana*
> City-girl, give in.

The Gaulish and mixed Gaulish-Latin inscription express similar sentiments, though often in stronger terms:

> *Geneta vis cara*
> Hello there sweet girl—are you willing?

> *Moni gnatha gabi buddutton imon*
> Come on girl, take my kiss.

However, the word translated as "kiss" (Gaulish *buddutton*) may in fact be related to Old Irish *bod* ("penis") and better translated as such.

In these inscriptions we once again see the popularity of drinking among the Gauls:

> *Nata uimpi pota vinum*
> Hey, pretty girl, drink some wine.

> *Nata uimpi curmi da*
> Hey beautiful, give me a beer!

Finally, a young woman responds to the advances in at least one inscription, suggesting no lack of self-confidence among Gaulish women:

> *Geneta imi daga uimpi*
> I'm a girl who is good and beautiful.

With the spread of Roman power throughout the Mediterranean world, the ancient Celtic languages were gradually overwhelmed and replaced by Latin. New inscriptions in the Celtic languages became less common and eventually ceased to be made as time passed. By the collapse of the western Roman Empire in the early fifth century A.D., few Celtic speakers survived in continental Europe. But in Roman Britain, as well as in unconquered Ireland, the Celtic languages survived to become the Welsh, Irish, Scottish Gaelic, and transplanted Breton of France still spoken today.

There is no shortage of books on the ancient Celts, but the quality and emphasis vary greatly.

There are a number of good general sources available on the Celts of ancient Europe. One of the best is Barry Cunliffe's *The Ancient Celts* (1997), a sound and very readable survey of early Celtic history and culture. A superb and extensive collection of essays by top Celtic scholars on everything from Celtic art and history to linguistics and weapons is found in *The Celtic World* (1995), edited by Miranda Green.

The best survey of Greek and Roman literary sources on the Celts is H. D. Rankin *Celts and the Classical World* (1987). Many of the classical texts as well as key medieval Irish and Welsh sources (all in translation) can be found in John Koch and John Carey *The Celtic Heroic Age* (2000). An excellent scholarly study of the Posidonian tradition is J. J. Tierney "The Celtic Ethnography of Posidonius" in *Proceedings of the Royal Irish Academy* 60C, no. 5 (1960, 189–275).

Three of the most sensible approaches to the ancient Druids are T. D. Kendrick *The Druids* (1966), Stuart Piggott *The Druids* (1975), and Miranda Green *The World of the Druids* (1997).

Those interested in early Celtic art can do no better than *The Celts* (1991), edited by Sabatino Moscati et al., and Ruth and Vincent Megaw *Celtic Art* (1989). Both books are copiously illustrated and provide a great deal of information on Celtic culture as well as artistic achievements.

S. Ireland *Roman Britain: A Sourcebook* (1992) is a comprehensive anthology of classical sources on ancient Britain. An excellent survey of archaeology in Ireland during the Greek and Roman era is Barry Raftery *Pagan Celtic Ireland* (1994), while the classical literary sources on Ireland are surveyed in my own *Ireland and the Classical World* (2001).

My chapter "The Ancient Celts Speak" requires a more detailed list of references and acknowledgments. I am particularly indebted to the work of those scholars who specialize in the ancient Celtic languages. An excellent survey of these languages, with full bibliography, may be found in "Continental Celtic" by Joseph Eska and D. Ellis Evans (*The Celtic Languages*, 1993, 26–63) edited by Martin Ball. For those interested in the details of Gaulish grammar, Pierre-Yves Lambert *La langue gauloise* (1994) is an important source.

The Lepontic inscriptions from Ornavasso and Vergiate can be found in Lambert (20–21), with the Cisalpine inscriptions from Todi and Vercelli in the same volume (71–79). Wolfgang Meid also reviews the Cisalpine evidence in his *Gaulish Inscriptions* (1992), but the definitive edition is *Recueil des inscriptions gauloises*, vol. II.1 (1988, 25–37, 41–52). The four volumes in this French series contain the most detailed and accurate collection of Gaulish inscriptions available.

The Galatian inscription from Egypt is #757 from W. Dittenberger, ed., *Orientis Graeci Inscriptiones Selectae* (1903–1905).

The Celtiberian inscription from Botorrita is carefully presented in Joseph Eska *Towards an Interpretation of the Hispano-Celtic Inscription of Botorrita* (1989) with detailed references. Wolfgang Meid provides a translation and analysis in *Celtiberian Inscriptions* (1994) of this and other Celtic inscriptions from Spain.

The Gaulish texts from Chamalières and Larzac are neatly presented in Lambert *La langue gauloise* (150–172) as well as in Koch and Carey *Celtic Heroic Age* (1–4). I am indebted to Lambert, Koch, and Meid (*Gaulish Inscriptions*, 38–46) for my own translations. A detailed survey of the Larzac tablet is also presented in Lejeune *La plomb magique du Larzac et les sorcières gauloises* (1986). The inscribed spindle-whorls are found in Lambert *La langue gauloise* (122–125) and Meid *Gaulish Inscriptions* (52–56).

INDEX